THE CHILD
HEALTHY
DIVORCE

ALSO BY ERICA KOMISAR

*Being There: Why Prioritising Motherhood
in the First Three Years Matters*

*Chicken Little the Sky Isn't Falling:
Raising Resilient Adolescents in the New Age of Anxiety*

ERICA KOMISAR

THE CHILD HEALTHY DIVORCE

How to Protect Your Child's Mental
and Emotional Health through a
Breakup or Separation

Cornerstone Press

CORNERSTONE PRESS

UK | USA | Canada | Ireland | Australia
India | New Zealand | South Africa

Cornerstone Press is part of the Penguin Random House group of companies whose addresses can be found at global.penguinrandomhouse.com

Penguin Random House UK,
One Embassy Gardens, 8 Viaduct Gardens, London SW11 7BW

penguin.co.uk

First published in the US by Countryman Press 2026
First published in the UK by Cornerstone Press 2026
001

Copyright © Erica Komisar, 2026

The moral right of the author has been asserted

Penguin Random House values and supports copyright.
Copyright fuels creativity, encourages diverse voices, promotes freedom of expression and supports a vibrant culture. Thank you for purchasing an authorised edition of this book and for respecting intellectual property laws by not reproducing, scanning or distributing any part of it by any means without permission. You are supporting authors and enabling Penguin Random House to continue to publish books for everyone. No part of this book may be used or reproduced in any manner for the purpose of training artificial intelligence technologies or systems. In accordance with Article 4(3) of the DSM Directive 2019/790, Penguin Random House expressly reserves this work from the text and data mining exception.

Printed and bound in Great Britain by Clays Ltd, Elcograf S.p.A.

The authorised representative in the EEA is Penguin Random House Ireland, Morrison Chambers, 32 Nassau Street, Dublin D02 YH68

A CIP catalogue record for this book is available from the British Library

ISBN: 978–1–529–95364–0

Penguin Random House is committed to a sustainable future for our business, our readers and our planet. This book is made from Forest Stewardship Council® certified paper.

To my incredible, loving husband, Jordan, whose encouragement and support made this book possible. Jordan, you are my best friend and the love of my life.

To my children, Bryce, Jonas, and Sofia, who are my biggest cheerleaders and fans.

And to my parents, Philip and Edith Komisar, who modeled every day a romantic marital relationship which endured through good times and adversity and provided my three sisters and me the emotional security we needed to grow and flourish.

CONTENTS

Introduction ix

1. A Good Divorce Is Better Than a Bad Marriage 1
2. Making a Plan That Puts Kids First 15
3. How to Talk to Your Ex and Your Child About Divorce 31
4. Legal Decisions, Emotional Consequences 45
5. What to Expect from Your Kid 59
6. Being Your Best Self as a Parent 73
7. Repairing Trust and Healing Trauma 93
8. New Partners and Blended Families 105
9. Special Situations 123
10. Is My Kid OK? 141
11. A Hopeful Note 157

Acknowledgments 167

Notes 169

Bibliography 181

Index 195

INTRODUCTION

MUCH OF MY PRACTICE as a therapist and parent guidance expert is devoted to trying to prevent pain that divorce can cause for children and to heal some of the unavoidable trauma. Parents who come to me learn how to prioritize their kids when they're divorcing and restore some sense of peace when a divorce goes wrong. I have learned a great deal through my thousands of hours of practice, how to put children's emotional health and well-being at the center of the process. This book shares with you the knowledge and wisdom gained from my more than 30 years of clinical practice. My two previous books focused on raising mentally healthy, resilient children, and this book does the same.

Substantial research provides evidence that marriage between two parents who love each other is the ideal way to raise kids. Marriage can make for hard work, but can also model what it takes to love someone over a lifetime for a child. If a marriage can be repaired and the love between two adults who have created a family can be rejuvenated, divorce isn't the answer. But sometimes two people can't resolve their differences in their relationship. In a family, chronic, intractable conflict does more harm to kids than a divorce embraced thoughtfully, sensitively, and empathetically.

This book offers a guide for you as a parent who wants to raise a healthy and resilient child, despite the stresses and upheaval of divorce. Doing so means transcending your own pain to focus on preventing and healing your kid's pain. It means the sacrifice of putting your child's needs and wants ahead of your own. Ideally, both you and your former partner will understand and adopt this philosophy, but even if you're dealing with a hostile, immature, and/or selfish ex, you can still make a difference.

Most people begin their parenting journey with love for each other, so it's in that spirit that I ask you to read this book. To prioritize your child properly, remember and respect the love that you once shared with your ex. Even if you share little else now, you continue to share your love for your child. That love is at the center of this book.

In the last three decades, we've learned so much about the importance of attachment security during the first three years of childhood, the first period of critical brain development. Infants and young children raised with the loving attention and the physical and emotional presence of their parents do better in the face of adversity, and divorce represents one of the biggest adverse experiences that kids can face.

Adolescence, which current neuroscience and developmental science recognizes as beginning around age 9 and ending around age 25, is the second critical period of brain development. In this phase, the second half of the attachment paradigm becomes more of an issue. For adolescents, divorce can feel uniquely threatening. The core process of adolescence is creating an identity separate from the parents. Adolescents, like toddlers, want and need present, sensitive, and empathic parents who will provide them with understanding and comfort. Disruptions to or destruction of that stability can feel traumatic, even for well-adjusted kids.

My advice and recommendations rest on the groundwork of decades of clinical experience and extensive research on the importance of attachment security and healthy separation to children's mental health. My goal is to give you tools to help you create a solid foundation of emotional security that sets your child on a successful course for life. Success doesn't mean just good grades or a good job; it means the ability to form strong personal ties, to nurture close friendships now and intimate relationships in the future.

Many of my colleagues have seen firsthand the damage that divorce can wreak on kids, so this book also offers guidance for other mental health professionals and faith-based counselors working with families struggling with the fallout of divorce. It aims to educate and support those in the legal system surrounding divorce: judges, attorneys, mediators, forensic psychologists, and parent coordinators. They all work tirelessly to help families resolve conflicts and find peace in an overwhelmed, oversubscribed system.

No one who has kids *wants* a divorce. But if divorce become a necessity, let's try to make it a healthier one that puts children first.

THE CHILD
HEALTHY
DIVORCE

1

A GOOD DIVORCE IS BETTER THAN A BAD MARRIAGE

Common wisdom holds that divorce is bad for kids. However, in bad marriages, children benefit when parents separate rather than expose them to seemingly endless hostility. Parents *can* negotiate this painful passage and cause as little harm to their kids as possible. On planes, flight attendants instruct you to put on your own oxygen mask first before helping others. In the same way, a child-healthy divorce puts children's needs and feelings first. It helps prevent kids from becoming collateral damage.

When you decide to share your life with another person and build a family, you think you're going to love each other and stay together forever. You want to provide a loving, secure home for your child. That's the dream, the ideal. But in America, half of marriages end in divorce. Second and third marriages fail at even higher rates: 60 and 70 percent, respectively.[1]

Many people think that couples shouldn't divorce because, for a growing child, an intact family offers the best environment—even if full of conflict. Today, much of that thinking comes from Judith Wallerstein's seminal *Second Chances: Men, Women & Children a Decade after Divorce,* published in 1989, and *The Unexpected Legacy of Divorce: The 25 Year Landmark Study*, published in 2004, which, beginning in 1971, followed 100 kids, age 3 to 18, of divorced parents.[2] Wallerstein's revolutionary books reported on the first longitudinal study to show the impact of divorce on children well after their parents split. These books concluded that, rather than recovering from the family breakup, these kids continued to suffer as adults. They had trouble at work, in romantic relationships, and as parents. The implication: *Stay in a bad marriage, no matter how difficult, for the good of the children.* But the thinking has changed.

Over the past decade or so, further studies have clarified the science, and parents have become more aware of the psychological impact of divorce on their children—and become more psychologically aware themselves. A Cornell University study published in 2009 found that adolescents who lived with parents who fought constantly were more likely to smoke, binge drink, and do poorly in school.[3] Another study published in 2019 noted that these children are "no better off, and in fact may fare worse in some respects, than children of single parents."[4] Research published by the Society for Research in Child Development found that "marital conflict is a significant source of environmental stress for children." It "may harm their stress response systems, affecting their mental and intellectual development" and "hinder children's development of cognitive ability."[5] A recent study published in *Hormone Research in Paediatrics* noted that childhood stress may increase the risk of neurodevelopmental disorders, such as autism spectrum disorder and ADHD.[6]

But here's some good news. Research also shows that, when parents provide warmth and emotional support and maintain age-appropriate expectations, children and adolescents can adjust in positive, healthy ways.[7]

Carmen Rodriguez, a mediator and collaborative lawyer at Rodriguez Law & Mediation, has seen that "What hurts the children isn't the divorce. It's the conflict." This shift in understanding not only helps children heal but can help you heal, too.

Jillian E. Gross, a founder and partner at Mosberg Sharma Stambleck

Gross, where she practices matrimonial law, has seen that "Parents tend to blur what's best for them and what's best for their children." Sometimes, it can prove challenging to distinguish what might satisfy your own need for equity and fairness with your ex and what lies in the best interest of your child; your child's interests and needs may differ from your own. Here's a good rule to remember: You will only be as happy as your least happy child.

The Bible story of King Solomon is a cautionary tale. Two mothers, each claiming a baby as her own, appeal to the king to judge their case. Solomon strategically orders the baby cut in half so each woman receives an equal share of the child. One woman agrees, but the other begs to spare the baby's life. Rather than see the child killed, she will relinquish the baby to the other woman. Solomon declares her the true mother because she put the child's life over her own desires. This parable accurately describes what happens every day in divorce courts: Parents face the challenge of doing what's right for their children, even if that conflicts with their own desires.

But, "Courts have moved away from this notion of there needing to be one primary figure," says Gross. This Bible story offers a lesson for divorcing parents and courts that decide custody. Children are not sandwiches and can't be split down the middle and shared equally. They do have a primary attachment figure, and each parent plays a unique role. Let's embrace progress when progress makes sense. Recognizing that fathers have rights and that mothers may not be primary caregivers or primary attachment figures for children marks an important step. Sometimes dads stay home to raise children, with mothers as primary wage earners. No matter how much we may want to see divorce as an issue of fairness and equity between parents, a good divorce focuses on what truly lies in the best interests of the child emotionally. A parent's willingness to sacrifice what seems fair for the parent can mean the difference between a child's becoming psychologically and emotionally stronger and resilient, or succumbing to the stress of the split and potentially falling prey to mental illness.

Children can heal from the trauma if parents proactively put aside their own pain and negative feelings and work together, in a neutral emotional space, to focus on their children's needs before, during, and after the divorce. Rodriguez tells her clients that "You need to parent together.... You are always going to be a family, but it's just going to be structured differently, and that's OK."

Conflict doesn't pose the only problem. In addition to modeling ongoing aggressive and disrespectful behavior, parents who stay in bad marriages aren't modeling love, an equally important consideration. When Wallerstein wrote her books, experts assumed the best-case scenario—parents respecting each other, resolving differences equitably, and repairing the relationship when necessary—as achievable. But without these ingredients, children don't learn how to function in loving, emotionally connected relationships. Parents' not expressing genuine affection toward each other and not respecting or trusting each other, creates a model for a life devoid of connection and intimacy. This situation can prove as hazardous and toxic to children as can extreme conflict. Again, divorce often offers the best path forward.

Even when parents recognize divorce as the right choice, when they have the best intentions, too often children become collateral damage in the ensuing tug of war. Adults, including lawyers and court officials, forget or ignore the emotional fragility and vulnerability of children, seeing parents as the only principals. The past four decades have seen an epidemic of mental health and behavioral disorders among children and adolescents. This developmental fragility comes into play when divorce upends families.

It doesn't matter whether children are age 3, 13, or 23. Parents have the responsibility to prevent, as much as possible, the trauma caused by divorce, to heal the wounds inevitable even in the best divorces, and to repair the bond of trust. Age does count, however, in terms of how much the breakup will affect kids. Timing of the split and the psychological developmental stage of the children also matter greatly, as do the parents' sensitivity to their children's feelings and reactions when they break the news and what they do to help the children cope.

Divorce Sucks for Everyone

Almost every day, as a parent guidance expert, I see children who have become casualties of acrimonious divorce. That's why the notion of a child-healthy divorce, which focuses on the mental and emotional health of the child, needs urgent, widespread implementation. With diagnoses of childhood depression, anxiety, and behavioral issues skyrocketing, it's the best way to protect and preserve children's mental health and help heal fractured parent-child relationships.

It can feel so hard to take care of others, especially those you love, when you are in pain yourself. Divorce brings up intense feelings: disappointment, loss, rejection, abandonment, betrayal, rage, sadness, and even depression. Joshua Foreman, a partner and family law attorney at Chemtob Moss Forman & Beyda, has seen that "divorce can trigger very selfish states." It often involves financial and social upheaval: loss of income, moving from the family home, clashing parenting styles, negotiating new family structures, and the logistics of shared custody. My work as a psychoanalyst compels me to share what I've learned about helping parents navigate marital conflict, divorce, and the aftermath.

A child-healthy split can prevent kids from becoming statistics, as we've seen. It also has tangible benefits for parents. In my practice, these strategies have yielded consistently positive results for many years. Patients tell me that it reduces stress between them and their ex, because it shifts focus from the failed marital relationship to the ongoing parent-child relationship. Gross finds that "Oftentimes a parent might see a divorce as a divorce of the family as opposed to a divorce of the parents." The strategies in this book not only can help parents bond with children again, but they also can help parents move on from the divorce more quickly.

CASE STUDY

After 16 years of marriage, Gary left Sarah for another woman. Sarah felt blindsided, so consumed with her own loss and anger that she couldn't see how the contentious divorce was affecting their son, Miles. At 13, Miles was dealing with the academic and social pressures of middle school. Sarah reported that he had been having panic attacks, and she suspected that he was self-medicating with marijuana easily available from other kids at school.

As much as Sarah wanted to help Miles, she couldn't imagine working with Gary on anything. It took time and convincing, but eventually she invited Gary to participate in parent guidance. They came to understand that, though a poor match in marriage, they could form a team to protect and build a healthy emotional future for their son. When Sarah stopped seeing herself as a victim and Gary acknowledged his feelings of guilt about his infidelity, they kept their conflicts to a minimum and coparented Miles successfully. They both communicated politely, if not warmly, removing negative and critical talk of each other, especially when they were with Miles. These steps resulted in easier transitions for Miles and a more flexible, supportive structure and routine for him that made their lives easier and less confrontational.

Separation or divorce may be the right choice and perhaps necessary for the safety of the children, but even an amicable divorce can shake the developmental foundation of a kid of any age, even young adults. For younger children, parents stand at the center of their universe. Older children and adolescents may seem more self-sufficient, but parents still have enormous importance and influence in their lives. They may not even know they're doing it, but adolescents—a life stage that lasts until age 25 or, in some cases, older, especially for young men—look to their parental relationships as a foundation on which to build their independence and as a model for their own intimate relationships. When parents divorce, children's trust in the stability and longevity of romantic relationships erodes, and their world can seem as if it's collapsing.

Attachment Security and Divorce

Neurological research has shown links between attachment security in early childhood (birth to age 3) and adult mental health.[8] This period of attachment lays the foundation for a lifetime of mental and emotional resilience. A child-centered divorce should pay special attention to this important period.

Children under age three are experiencing a critical period of brain development in which their environment, such as an unstable home, has an outsize effect on development.[9] Equally shared custody for kids under that age isn't best for their mental health. The primary caregiver or attachment figure should have primary custody, with the other parent having visitation rights rather than overnight custody. A study from the University of Virginia, looking at how joint custody affected infant attachment to the parents, found that children who spent a night way from the primary parent had a less secure attachment to them.[10] A strong bond with one parent was better than weak bonds with two. Another study from University of Iowa found that, if a child doesn't develop a strong bond with a parent before age two, that weak or missing bond increases the risk of the child developing emotional issues later. Having a strong bond with one parent decreased the chance.[11]

Babies and toddlers rely almost exclusively on their primary attachment figure, usually the mother, to soothe their distress on demand, which protects and buffers them from stress and provides a feeling of safety.[12] After age three, they can internalize that feeling so that, when the primary caregiver isn't physically present, they can still summon it mentally for comfort. As children grow, they need the secondary parent, usually the father, to help them with separation and feeling comfortable exploring the world. But kids of any age, even through adolescence, need the reassurance of touching base with their primary attachment figure to help with regulating stress and emotions.

CASE STUDY

Taylor and John courted for only a short time before they wed, and after a year of marriage, they conceived their daughter, Anne. Taylor soon realized that John was a workaholic. He spent long hours at the office and traveled frequently for work. John supported Taylor's decision to stay home with their daughter, but his expectation for Taylor's independence didn't match her need for his attention and affection. As he stayed away more, she became angry, restless, and resentful. When they realized that their marriage had been a mistake, Anne was 11 months old. A sensitive baby, she was breastfed exclusively and loved contact naps and co-sleeping with Taylor when John was away.

When Taylor and John came to see me, John angrily demanded fifty-fifty custody with Anne, including overnight visitation. It wasn't fair, he said, for him not to have equal time with his daughter—despite that he didn't plan to modify his work or travel schedule. He planned to hire a live-in nanny, and his mother would stay with him from time to time to help with childcare.

John didn't realize that his anger and possessiveness could threaten Anne's emotional security. With my help, the couple learned about the importance of attachment security and how disrupting that attachment could create immediate problems and later consequences. As their daughter grew, developed a greater sense of security, and naturally separated from her mother, the situation would change, I told them. However, at this stage, John needed to make a sacrifice so Anne could benefit in the long term.

Taylor and John negotiated a custody agreement that felt fair to them both and, most important, whose terms were in Anne's best interests. Anne would continue to sleep at Taylor's home, and Taylor would wean her between 14 and 18 months of age. John reduced his travel schedule, and Taylor agreed that he could spend as much time with their daughter as he wanted during the day, at home, and put her to bed on some of the nights when he wasn't traveling. The couple also agreed that Anne wouldn't sleep at her father's home for the time being. After Taylor weaned Anne, they would implement a nesting arrangement, once per week for up to one year: Once a week, John would sleep at Taylor's home, and Taylor would stay elsewhere. When Anne was two and half *and* if she seemed ready to both parents, she could sleep at her father's home. If a trial sleepover went well, they would revisit the custody schedule and continue to adapt to their daughter's changing needs.

When children are infants and toddlers, parents feel most insecure about their love and most possessive over the right to spend time with them. Regardless of whether they mean to, parents communicate this insecurity and anxiety to their kids, who already are struggling with feelings of divided loyalties. These ingredients can create a perfect storm that puts children at risk at this age and in the future.

Adolescence marks the second sensitive period of brain development in which divorce affects kids more intensely.[13] At this stage, emotionally vulnerable teens need a stable environment so they can separate from their parents in a healthy way. Parents divorcing right before children go to college or move out of the family home can become one of the most challenging times for kids. Adolescents practice independence by exploring the world with their friends. They come home to their parents to refill their emotional fuel tanks before venturing out again. It's hard to feel secure in the world when home base is crumbling.

Divorce Has Changed

Half a century ago, couples couldn't divorce easily, and custody and financial agreements had far less flexibility. Today, divorces look quite different. Many states have no-fault divorce laws that allow either parent to initiate proceedings without cause. The legalization of same-sex marriage has led to more varied configurations of families. Technology has increased how people can become parents through in-vitro fertilization (IVF), donors, and surrogacy. Some five million children live with parents who aren't married.[14] A couple not legally bound may not go through the same legal processes, but the practical and emotional issues remain. All these elements can complicate uncoupling.

Today, both parents often work outside the home, and both often raise their children. Custody doesn't go automatically to the mother or primary caregiver. In recent years, determining the primary caregiver is frequently decided by the court. Over his 25 years in the business, Foreman has found that "people have begun to care more about the kids, and dads really want to spend more time with their kids than ever before." With a rise in the number of stay-at-home fathers, alimony and even child support don't have the same guarantees that they once did, and they no longer align along gender or traditional roles.

More accessible than ever, the divorce process ironically can prove harder to complete. According to Judith L. Poller, matrimonial attorney and cochair of Pryor Cashman's Family Law Group, "It takes two years to get to trial" in worst-case scenarios. The more divorces in the system, the more overwhelmed the system becomes, and there aren't enough judges to address the number of cases that need negotiating.

Modern divorces often take years from start to finish. "Even in a case where you just have to file the divorce paperwork, purely clerical work, you can wait up to a year," Gross says. The length of the process has increased the stress that families feel. Divorces aren't always consensual and can result in one or both parents feeling hurt and angry, leading to breakdowns in communication and civility. Children can suffer acute or chronic emotional trauma from being deposed or called to speak with a judge. Issues around custody and finances can persist beyond legal proceedings, too. Kids may have to change schools or leave friends and a familiar neighborhood. They may have to separate from beloved grandparents or cousins.

Changing configurations of families have made the process more complicated and harder to negotiate as well. Gender equality, same-sex marriage, new ways to have children (donors, surrogacy), changing family structures, and the rising number of adoptions all have made legal precedents a moving target.

With movement toward gender neutrality, courts bend over backward in the name of fairness when granting custody or making decisions about the logistics of custody. "There isn't sensitivity to the theory of attachment security," Gross says, echoing my experience. Breastfeeding mothers send me frantic emails begging for help to prevent courts from awarding fifty-fifty physical custody to their exes, including sleepovers. "Judges don't have enough of the right education around mental health to understand what's best for the kids," says Poller. Courts ignore that children are neurologically fragile, rapidly developing human beings with a primal need for emotional security. Sensitivity to the primary attachment figure, particularly in the first three years, matters critically to their emotional and mental health.

All these details complicate the process for everyone. Today, with the inclusion of parent coordinators and forensic psychologists, divorce courts attempt to consider the best interests of the children, but parental interests still widely drive the process, rather than what's right for the kids. Many overwhelmed judges see custody as a fairness issue for parents, and that's it. You'd think we would've learned more from King Solomon.

Timing

Parents often ask: When's the best time to divorce? Much of the time, you can't or shouldn't delay it, but waiting until a youngest child turns three works better for kids. Unfortunately, that's not always possible, but you can make it easier. Here's another way to answer the question. The best time is when living together without constant and unresolvable conflict is no longer possible. In a perfect world, everyone would split with kids between ages three and nine, the most stable period of brain development for children.

During these years, children focus on building social skills, cognitive learning in school, and developing interests and competencies that may shape their personalities in adolescence. It's like the eye of the hurricane or an oasis in the desert. The other relatively "safe" period comes after adolescence, when kids have launched successfully from home base to their own homes and emotional support systems outside the family. At this time, a divorce is less likely to become part of their personal narrative or define their personalities. A thoughtfully timed divorce not only can mitigate harmful effects on children, but it can help build emotional resilience.

CASE STUDY

After the birth of their second daughter, Jane and Bill realized that they couldn't reconcile their differing interests and outlooks on life. Jane loved the outdoors and wanted to live in the country; Bill loved the city and hated nature. Jane had strong faith and attended church regularly; Bill detested religion and had no use for spirituality. Jane loved spending time with their kids; Bill preferred to play golf on Saturdays instead of attending the girls' weekend activities and thought parent teacher conferences a waste of time. The couple had become chalk and cheese. Each felt abandoned and betrayed by the other. Unable to control their anger, they couldn't sit in the same room without fighting. They decided to divorce and came to me for help with telling their daughters, Samantha, age 6, and Cam, age 2, in a way that focused on the girls' needs and made the process easier for them.

Samantha—more sensitive and more aware of the tension between her parents—was suffering. When her parents argued, she wore a pair of old earmuffs and retreated to a corner. She withdrew more and more. Interactions with her parents devolved to yes-or-no answers, and she ignored her sister. She also isolated herself from other kids at school, not participating in class and ignoring invitations from classmates for playdates or birthday parties. Cam, still a toddler, clung constantly to her mother and threw tantrums when Jane left the house, even when her father was there. Cam cried inconsolably when her mother dropped her off at preschool.

Jane and Bill needed to acknowledge the elephant in the room. Their fighting was stressing *everyone*. They agreed to put Samantha in play therapy to help her express and work through her feelings of sadness, fear, and anger. Cam was too young for therapy, so Jane and Bill worked to reflect her feelings and put them into words that she could understand.

Despite their own hurt and animosity, Jane and Bill both wanted emotional stability for their girls. Their daughters' mental health became their guiding light during the rocky transition to their new reality. On my recommendation, Jane and Bill decided to delay the divorce until after Cam had turned three. During that time, I helped them prepare for their coparenting relationship. With that timing in mind, they talked to the girls

> about the love that they had shared when they were first married. They acknowledged that, sometimes, adults' relationships change and they parent better while living apart. Accepting that they were divorcing also allowed Jane and Bill to treat each other with more respect for the year they stayed together.

Now that you understand a child-healthy divorce, let's make a plan to lay the foundation for a divorce that prioritizes and protects your child.

2

MAKING A PLAN THAT PUTS KIDS FIRST

Most parents want the best for their children and begin the process of divorcing with good intentions. They want to protect the children and do what's right for them. Unfortunately, many fall prey to the pitfalls of divorce: hostility, possessiveness, jealousy, envy, and insecurity. In my clinical experience, only rarely has a parent deliberately acted to hurt a child or weaponize a kid to hurt the other parent. Most parents act from love. But even with the best of intentions, children too often become collateral damage in the ensuing tug of war.

You need to create a plan that puts your children's needs before your own, and the child's age matters. For children younger than age nine, parents stand at the center of their universe. Divorce collapses that world. Adolescents may seem more self-sufficient, but research has shown the importance and influence of parents in their lives.[1] Teens look to their parents for a foundation on which to build their own independence. It's easier to jump off a stable diving board than a broken one.

Creating your plan begins with assessing your situation, building your support system, and acting with awareness and composure, rather than selfishness and anger. To create the plan, Corey M. Shapiro, a divorce attorney in New York City, puts it best: "Be willing to believe in the process." As Carmen Rodriguez says, start "by grounding yourself back to what's important: the child and the impact on the child." Both parents should put aside feelings of rejection, anger, or abandonment to help their kids heal and build resilience. Protecting your children means being your best selves first and a willingness to sacrifice your own desires to put your children's needs before your own. As I remind parents in my practice, kids didn't ask for the divorce, so don't punish them for it. "The children didn't make any choices," says Joshua Foreman. "They were made by the parents, and they're stuck with their choices."

Being Your Best Self

Wellness and productivity gurus talk a lot about being your best self. But what does that mean in this context? It starts with self-awareness and reflection. It means being emotionally secure and having a solid sense of self-esteem. It means suspending the hurt that your partner may have caused or the guilt from hurt that you may have caused, and sidelining any desire to retaliate. It means putting your children's well-being before your own.

Easier said than done, I understand, especially given that, in this context, many people experience compound losses or traumas: the death of a grandparent, a difficult relationship with or death of a parent, rejection by a romantic partner, financial difficulty, discrimination, and so on. For many adults, divorce can exacerbate or reopen those painful wounds. Past losses or other suffering combined with the emotional ordeal of divorce can feel utterly overwhelming.

You need to regulate and process your own emotions so you can help your child regulate and process theirs.[2] If you're feeling mentally depleted, emotionally fragile, or psychologically vulnerable, you risk displacing your anger and pain onto your kid. Make time to care for yourself: Meditate, exercise, socialize, or engage in healthy activities that nourish you and give you joy. Create a support system of family and/or friends who can empathize and offer good, practical, logistical support. If you haven't already, find a therapist who can help you work through your anger, sadness, and other emotions. Most people need help resolving those feelings, which means that most divorcing parents do, too. Don't be a martyr. You don't get a prize for going it alone. Seek help.

In a divorce, parents and children commonly feel anger. But it's hard to exercise constructive awareness of that anger, to understand where it's coming from, and to recognize where it's going or should go. The stress of divorce doesn't bring out anyone's best, parent or child, and it can prove hard to distinguish feelings of hostility and resentment toward your ex from similar feelings of conflict with your child. It's all too easy to react or overreact to something that your child does or says when you're actually upset with your ex—as Sheila and Mark's story attests.

CASE STUDY

Sheila and Mark divorced when their son Spencer, a high-energy child, was eight. Mark drank heavily, so the court gave Sheila primary custody, though he had generous visitation rights. But he rarely showed up when he said he would, changed plans with little notice, and often cut short visits with his son. That behavior infuriated Sheila and deeply upset Spencer. The unpredictability and stress created more friction in their home. Sheila loved Spencer, but she also resented him for the care that he required, particularly when she felt tired and that she had little space for herself in her own life.

Sheila had several conferences with Spencer's teachers to discuss his inattention and distractibility in class, which worsened during the divorce. At home, he needed much of her attention. When he couldn't control himself or ignored her, she yelled

> at him or spanked him. She almost immediately regretted her reaction, feeling guilty and remorseful.
>
> Sheila knew that her impatience and anger toward Spencer wasn't really about him. She wanted to vent her feelings to Mark and have him change his behavior, but she also knew that desire wasn't realistic. Therapy gave her a place and the tools to deal with those feelings, which in turn gave her more patience and energy for dealing with her son. She also made a point to have close friends on speed-dial and to get together with them for a willing ear and a shoulder to lean on when she felt overwhelmed.

Having people in your corner—whether paid advisers, supportive friends, or empathetic family—will help protect you and your family as emotional, financial, legal, and other issues arise. Establish or strengthen that network *before* discussing divorce with your spouse. Think of it like camping: You need to have a plan and the right resources before heading into the wilderness.

Building Your Support System

Support comes in many shapes and sizes: family, friends, coworkers, and professionals such as therapists, an attorney or mediator, a trusted financial adviser, a parent coordinator for negotiating coparenting concerns in the future, and support groups. Here are the basics.

First, who do you want in your circle of trust? Not everyone, even your closest relatives or dear friends, may support your best interests. A parent or sibling might offer more criticism than encouragement. A coworker might keep turning the conversation back to her own experiences instead of trying to help you process yours. A friend might feel torn between supporting you or your spouse. Take some time to think about your relationships with people whom you might tap for your support network. If you're not sure, don't be afraid to reach out to your inner circle to let them know you're going to need extra support and TLC during your divorce. You'll know who you can rely on. Interview them for the role of supporter in time of need.

While you're doing that, line up professional advisers. Many decisions that you'll be making will impact more than one part of your life: emotions, finances, home, the legal process of the divorce itself, and your children.

Both parents and children can benefit enormously from seeing a therapist, ideally once the divorce begins and for a while after it's final. Rodriguez always encourages her clients to "bring in a mental health expert." A good, unbiased, objective therapist doesn't carry the agendas, unconscious or otherwise, that friends and family might. Your therapy also protects your children by letting you process your feelings and vent in private so those feelings don't spill onto them. With telehealth appointments through various video conference apps, therapy has become more accessible than ever. Getting that help is easier and less expensive now, even for those without insurance.

When it comes to finding a therapist for your child, look for different types of therapy, depending on the child's age. For children between the ages of 3 and 12, play or art therapy is the best approach. Around age 12 or 13, most children can articulate their emotions, at which point talk therapy can be more effective. If a child of this age or older is less verbal or has trouble expressing feelings in words, a cognitive behavioral therapist (CBT) or dialectical behavior therapist (DBT) may be able to help.

If your child seems to be handling the situation well, you can wait before engaging the services of a therapist, but still research types of treatment and providers early so you can move quickly if necessary. Follow your kid's cues. If you see clear signs of stress—which could include meaningful changes in behavior, altered sleep patterns, issues at school, or isolating from friends—schedule an appointment right away. Therapy will give your child a safe, neutral space to deal with feelings without worrying about hurting you or your ex. Child therapists frequently offer parent guidance as well, which teaches parenting skills and focuses on improving parent-child interactions. Most emotional and mental health issues in children result from family dynamics, so if you send a child to therapy without participating in parent guidance yourself, you're doing only half the work. If your child's therapist doesn't do parent guidance, ask for a referral to a therapist for you who does. Your pediatrician, hospital website, child's school, and divorced friends can serve as good sources of information in this area.

If finances are a concern, you may be able to find providers who charge on a sliding scale based on income. Psychotherapy and psychoanalytic training institutes, which exist in most big cities, frequently have low-fee referral services. At psychoanalytic training institutes, the well-trained therapists already have many years of experience in their field.

Timing Is (Almost) Everything

As we saw in the previous chapter, the most challenging times for children to experience divorce take place during the two critical periods of their social-emotional brain development.[3] The first occurs between birth and age three, when brains are growing rapidly.[4] The second happens during adolescence, which lasts from age 9 to 25. During adolescence, the brain prunes unnecessary synapses—the connections between neurons—which is essential for healthy brain development.[5] During these two periods, children have a heightened sensitivity to stress and their environment, which shapes the brain's architecture.[6] Emotional security paired with minimal conflict support their long-term mental health and personality development.[7] This information doesn't mean that you shouldn't divorce during this time, but that you need to exercise sensitivity and empathy regarding your kid's emotional needs when thinking about timing the split.

For a child from birth to age three, the primary caregiver or attachment figure should have primary custody. For the other parent, that means daytime visitation but no overnight visits. This arrangement may not feel fair, seeming to favor one parent over the other, but with good reason. Emotional security, the foundation of mental health, connects directly to attachment security.[8] Nighttime security, having the primary attachment figure present at night for comfort, matters as much if not more than daytime security.[9] The primary attachment figure takes on most of the physical and emotional care of a child. This person often oversees key daily transitions—waking in the morning; drop-offs and pickups for daycare, preschool, or playdates; bedtime; waking in the middle of the night—and offers comfort in times of distress. Abruptly forcing separation from this person can harm a child's sense of security. A University of Virginia study looked at how joint custody affected an infant's attachment to the parents. It found that children who spent a night way from the primary parent had a less secure attachment to that parent and that a strong bond with one parent was better than weak bonds with two.[10] Another study from the UK found that, if a child doesn't develop a strong bond with a parent before age two, that increases the risk of emotional issues in the future. Having a strong bond with one parent decreased that chance.[11]

Many parents who I treat wait to divorce until their children reach their teens, believing incorrectly that their children need them less emotionally because they're becoming more independent. Divorcing when your children are still going through the process of separating from you and establishing adult lives of their own prevents them from refueling or experiencing what psychiatrist Margaret Mahler called "rapprochement,"[12] the back and forth between independence and natural and normal dependence on parents, which mirrors the same process in toddlers.

Between ages three and nine, kids have passed the tantrum stage, accepting structure and limits, learning to become competent and confident, and developing their own world of friends (whom they'll need as their own support system during the divorce). The hormone surges and mood swings of adolescence aren't plaguing them yet. At this stage, kids also feel more ready to spend more time with the nonprimary caregiver. In certain developmental periods, one parent proves more important than another, but in adolescence, kids need *both* parents.

For timing, also consider your child's experiences of other losses—injury, ill health, social problems, academic difficulties, moving the family home, death in the family, and so on—and emotional or neurological sensitivity, which may compound stress. Weigh the harm of delaying the divorce against the challenges that your child is already facing. This equation has no easy answers, but carefully evaluating it helps put your child's well-being at the heart of your decision-making process, which is our goal here.

Change as Little as Possible, as Slowly as Possible

In the beginning, introduce as little change as possible to your child's life and make gradual changes to the schedule and environment over time. Think of weaning a baby: You slowly lengthen the time between feedings and/or decrease feeding time, while introducing other forms of nourishment and comfort. A child-healthy divorce keeps children's lives as much the same as possible: the same bedroom, residence, childcare arrangements, and school. The primary caregiver of a new baby, rather than making the baby accommodate, molds to the baby's shape to provide comfort, security, and protection. Remember that model. Change inevitably comes, but you can buffer the effects and prevent unnecessary stress by explaining to your child what will happen, listening, and giving enough time for adjustment to new routines. Now is not the time for more surprises or ignoring feelings, fears, or concerns.

After separating, parents with children under age five should set up a nesting arrangement for 6 to 12 months. "Nesting" means that your child remains at the primary residence and the parents alternate living there. Again, think of it as weaning. It's not a long-term solution; it provides children with time to adjust. Nesting works best with amicable or reasonably amicable divorces.

Unfortunately, many couples can't manage this arrangement for long, because conflicts and negative feelings become too intense. In that case, one parent should live with the children at the primary residence, and the other parent finds another place to live. In the beginning, the children should spend time with each parent separately. Ideally, at each parent's home, they will have a room of their own or a dedicated space for toys, clothes, books, and anything else that offers comfort. When children feel comfortable, they can sleep there. But when making arrangements, listen to, consider, and respect their wishes. Their words or their actions will let you know when they're ready for overnights.

Older children should maintain as many of the same routines and familiar relationships as possible: attending the same school, participating in the same extracurricular activities, having the same family or childcare support, partaking in the same religious observances, and so on.

Give Your Child Some Control

How much control should kids have over decisions that affect them? Until they leave home, children have little control of their lives. They didn't choose to be born, and they didn't choose your divorce. Children given some control over their lives from an early age have stronger emotional health than those not given the same power.[13] Having choices helps them with self-control, self-discipline, and individual agency.[14] But the choices must be age appropriate, and too many can feel overwhelming.

Toddlers have fewer tantrums if, within reason, they can choose what they want in some areas of life. "For breakfast, do you want eggs or waffles?" "Do you want to wear the green pants or the blue ones?" As kids grow older, they need, and you can give them, more control over more consequential choices. A 10-year-old can decide whether to play soccer or take piano lessons. A 13-year-old can choose between summer camp or staying home and finding projects to do around the house and hanging out with neighborhood friends. A 16-year-old can decide to ride to school with friends or take the bus. When children turn 18, they gain control of their own actions and, with that, the responsibility for their decisions and the consequences. Until then, parents ultimately remain in control of the big decisions: vaccinations, schooling, curfews, and so on.

It may seem absurd to say that 18-year-olds can make big life decisions by themselves, but that's the law. After your child turns 18, you can't speak separately with their doctors without their written permission. In rare cases—usually unbearable home situations with unhinged parents—children as young as 16 can petition the court for emancipation, meaning legal independence, from their parents. In those unusual instances, they can make decisions about their own living arrangements.

When parents divorce, kids feel that they have no choice in what's happening to their family. Giving them a voice in at least some decisions that affect them can make them feel more empowered and less out of control. If your child feels uncomfortable spending the night in Dad's new apartment or says that she's not ready to see it yet, don't force the issue—even if it hurts Dad's feelings. Think of it as a jammed window: Forcing it can break the glass, but handling it with care can resolve the jam without causing damage. Trust your child's decisions and process of adapting to the new living situation. If they want to spend an extra night at your ex's apartment, giving them that flexibility will strengthen *your* relationship with your kid. Ignoring what they want only reinforces that they have no control over their lives and that you don't care about their feelings.

Offer them choices with limits, however. Indulging them too much and providing too many choices can trigger anxiety. Children feel safe when given clear, firm, gentle, flexible boundaries. Give them a say in after-school activities or their not participating in any, in what they wear and eat, and other decisions that do not involve their health and/or safety. Ask for their input on where to go on vacation or how to decorate their room. They have no say over your friendships, love life, work schedule, matters of health and safety, or household finances. You may choose to talk to them about those topics, but there the final say is yours.

It's all about balance. Giving children some control doesn't mean that they rule the household. Because divorce makes parents feel guilty, many comply with unreasonable requests and demands. "Kids manipulate the parents just like parents manipulate the kids," says Foreman. Children of divorce often use material objects—toys, games, clothes, trips, and more—as proof of parental love and to feel empowered. Kids can become quite adept at playing one parent against the other.

Parents often use material goods to substitute for time and attention. Don't fall into this trap and don't let your child confuse your love and attention with stuff. This confusion can interrupt the development of your child's self-esteem and their future relationships and career choices. It's hard to uncross crossed emotional wires. Remember that your kids want your love, time, and attention not your money, possessions, and resources—even if they ask for or demand them.

Anticipating Conflicts and Needs

You can't anticipate all your children's needs and questions, but let's address a few that may seem less obvious.

Kids worry about money. Many women, who often have primary or sole custody, find themselves significantly less well off after a divorce. A study published by the US Government Accountability Office found that women's household income fell an average of 41 percent after divorce.[15] The US Census reported that fewer than half of custodial parents received the full child support due to them.[16] Both parties should seek professional financial advice when divorcing—especially stay-at-home moms, who have rights that they may not know or understand. Plenty of accountants and financial advisers specialize in exactly this area.

Don't share your financial anxieties with your children. The more anxious you seem, the more anxious they'll become. The younger the child, the less hard information and more reassurance you need to provide. You can share more information with older children, but even young adults look to their parents for assurance that everything will be OK. This doesn't mean you can't share new financial constraints, within reason. If you need support or to vent, share with your friends or a therapist, not your kids.

Kids also worry about the routines and environments that make them feel safe. They may ask about their living situation, school, family pets, and neighborhood friends before thinking about custody arrangements. If that happens, don't take it personally or feel insulted. They're thinking: *Can I live my life as I know it without change? What am I going to lose, and what should I prepare for?* Don't promise that nothing will change, if that's not the case. Be honest if adjustments in vacations, gifts, eating out, or shopping are coming, but don't overshare.

Even in amicable divorces, conflict is inevitable. Many mothers have a "spidey sense" about accidents, a hypervigilance about protecting their children. If they see a glass on the edge of the counter, they usually move it because they can see the accident before it happens. In the same way, try to anticipate conflicts that may occur between you and your ex. Deal with them promptly rather than waiting until they become explosive. If you know that your birthday falls on a weekend when your ex has custody and you want to spend that time with your kids, don't wait until the week before to discuss the schedule, and don't make promises if don't know you can keep them. If you're fine with your eight-year-old's sleeping at a friend's house but your ex isn't, resolve that disagreement *before* the situation arises—even if the outcome makes your child unhappy. That kind of strategic planning will take the pressure off both parents and give kids time to adjust.

The Three Ps

As you go through your divorce, always keep in mind two tools and a goal: pause, perspective, and peace of mind—the three Ps.

Pause

Sometimes, past experiences, emotions, and instincts trigger strong reactions. Divorce can elicit sadness, anger, frustration, and fear, all normal and expected in the process. Parents and kids alike lose their tempers and say things that they may regret later.

Take a step back to identify what you're feeling and why.[17] If you feel upset or angry, pause before you speak to your kid or ex. That may mean counting to 10, rescheduling an appointment for later in the day or week, or consciously delaying a decision until your head clears. As talk show host Bernard Meltzer said, "Before you speak, ask yourself if what you are going to say is true, is kind, is necessary, is helpful. If the answer is no, then maybe what you are about to say should be left unsaid."[18] What's necessary or helpful may not be kind, but it still may need saying. Taking time to think about *how* to say something can defuse a volatile situation. Avoiding defensiveness and aggression can help protect you and your child from the negativity of divorce.

Pausing allows you first to decide whether a conversation or decision needs to happen at that moment. How either of those will affect your child's emotional well-being can serve as a useful litmus test. If something doesn't support your child's best interests, is it the right decision? Second, it affords you the time to formulate the best way to phrase what you need to say.

Regulating strong emotions models that behavior for your child. Blowing up at every provocation, deliberate or otherwise, teaches your kid that it's acceptable to do the same, which you don't want to do. Moderating your emotions represents the greatest tool that you have for preventing and deescalating arguments.

Perspective

Perspective requires distance from strong emotions. Like children, adults can struggle with regulating emotions, particularly after trauma or loss. When hurt, you may not feel like your most mature, adult self. Anger, rejection, abandonment, rage, and sadness can erode your ability to separate strong feelings from thoughts and actions, in turn interfering with critical objectivity about saying and doing what's best for your child. Giving yourself time before you speak or act gives you a better chance of not transferring your own pain and distress onto their shoulders.

Divorce is a marathon, not a sprint. Don't sweat little details unless, if left unattended, they'll create bigger problems. Reacting to every small or unimportant-in-the-long-term issue sets a contentious, confrontational tone that can prolong or complicate an already complicated process. "What a good attorney, therapist, or mediator does," says Shapiro, "is help you take a step back and slow it down." If you can stand back, not see every argument as a struggle for your self-worth, and decide which disagreements genuinely matter, you'll have a greater chance of successfully negotiating truly important disputes.

Peace of Mind

The third P represents your ultimate goal, but let's face it—peace of mind and divorce rarely go hand in hand. Constant conflict, irreconcilable differences, and emotional chaos often precede a permanent rupture. Many couples live in this state for *years*. Our bodies and minds have ways to handle normal, acute (short-term) stress. Long-standing conflicts, on the other hand, create chronic stress. Overtaxed and overwhelmed systems for regulating stress eventually will break down and cease to work.

Chronic stress can contribute to emotional and mental disorders such as addiction, depression, anxiety, and even psychotic episodes.[19] In the short term, divorce can worsen existing conditions, such as depression and anxiety. For Judith L. Poller, there's "no question in my mind that the hardest thing for kids is the experience of the conflict between the parents." After the divorce finalizes, the dissipation of that aggression can increase kids' acceptance of new family configurations. Some of the children of divorce whom I've treated suffered from depression with suicidal thoughts or behavioral issues at home and school. When the terms of the divorce were settled and life became calm—again or for the first time—those symptoms and conditions often resolved.

Chronic stress also can trigger physical breakdowns, including illness.[20] During a protracted divorce, one parent I treated developed chronic fatigue syndrome. Another was diagnosed with breast cancer. Research hasn't demonstrated a direct connection between stress and cancer or other diseases, but it has shown that chronic stress suppresses the immune system, leaving the body more vulnerable to illness.[21] We often think of mind and body separately, but they connect in such a way that chronic stress can activate previously inactive genetic switches for disease.

Deciding to divorce can feel like a tremendous relief, especially if you've experienced uncertainty or ambivalence about taking that step. As disruptive as divorce may be for parents and children alike, it can lead to calmer, more peaceful interactions and coparenting in the future by providing closure and resolution. Talking to an objective professional, such as a therapist, attorney, or parent coordinator, can help you make decisions in your and your child's best interests.

CASE STUDY

Soon after Kate and Paul had their first child, James, they realized that their interests and values didn't align. They associated James with the breakdown of their marriage, but they also thought that having more kids would heal their fractured bond. By the time they came to me, they had had three: James, 13, Susan, 7, and Mitchell, 5. The situation improved when Kate was pregnant with the younger two and when all the kids were very young, but it became clear that divorce would serve everyone's best interests.

As a couple, Kate and Paul had suffered for years. The split affected James most. He was struggling at school and quit the basketball team, which he loved. Visibly sad and depressed, he withdrew from friends and teachers. At my suggestion, he went into individual therapy, where he confessed that, though he knew the divorce made good sense, he still felt responsible for his parents' unhappiness and was angry at their "selfishness" of having so many children impacted by "the mess they had made." All three kids, even little Mitchell, knew how unhappy their parents felt. Therapy gave James a safe place to mourn the end of

> his parents' marriage and the dissolution of the family unit. But he saw that, apart, his parents grew happier and behaved civilly to each other while coparenting. Eventually he accepted and embraced his family's new reality. He also expressed relief at living in a less hostile, conflict-filled environment.

Because every family situation differs, no single plan will fit all possibilities, but you now have a solid framework with which to craft in individual, personalized plan to ease the transition to this new phase of life for your child.

3

HOW TO TALK TO YOUR EX AND YOUR CHILD ABOUT DIVORCE

Conflicts and misunderstanding plague communication during divorce. You need to temper honesty with restraint and decide what information to share or withhold if it will cause harm. Containment—the psychological term for absorbing and interpreting your child's emotions—must temper unfiltered emotion. Listen more than you speak. Show sensitivity to emotional cues and provide enough age-appropriate information for reassurance without overwhelming. It's a hard line to walk. If your teenager starts scrolling or your toddler wanders away while you're talking, take a break and try again later. Expressing your feelings matters, but don't burden your child with your pain or fears.

How you talk about your divorce with your ex and your child can go a long way to helping everyone adjust to the new reality. It can protect your child or cause hurt. It can make your ex a working, amicable coparent or result in alienation. The choice is yours.

When to Tell Your Child

Children are smarter than you think. Infants and toddlers can sense tension and discord, and kids know when their parents aren't getting along. If they have friends at school or cousins who are going through or have gone through divorce, they'll be more sensitized to the possibility. That's why, when parents fight, even over little things, kids often ask: "Are you getting a divorce?"

The best time to tell your child that you're divorcing is when you're ready to begin the physical process. Before you make the decision, do your due diligence first. See individual therapists and a couple's therapist. Talk to a mediator or lawyer, to understand all the implications and ramifications. Don't announce that you're divorcing unless you're going through with it. Once you shatter your kid's worldview of having a "happy" family, you can't undo it. Even if you reconcile, that announcement will wound a child's trust and shake feelings of security and safety to their foundation.

Give your child enough time to process the information while taking the next steps in the process. Other than staying at the party too long, forcing children to live in constant conflict, the next hardest thing for kids is when parents yo-yo, behave ambivalently about leaving, and involve children too early in the decision-making process. Imagine how confusing it must seem to learn that your parents are splitting but they keep sleeping in the same room or even bed. If nothing changes after the conversation, you've made the announcement too soon. Have a clear plan in place that includes any new sleeping arrangements *and* an exit strategy from the family home for one of you: another residence or staying with a friend or other family until you can figure out more permanent living arrangements.

On the other hand, don't make the announcement on the same day that one of you moves out. Again, give your child enough time to process the information: one week or two at most unless there are extenuating circumstances, such as significant illness in the immediate family, holidays, birthdays, or other meaningful occasions occurring on or close to a parent's departure.

Finding the Right Time

There's no getting around telling your child, and it'll be one of the most difficult conversations that you and your ex ever have. Steer clear of important events: birthdays, major holidays, school celebrations, and the like. You don't want your kid to associate the divorce with those events. Take into account important tests or school performances, which already come with anxiety, and other major stressors, such as illness, the death of a beloved family member or pet, or, for teens, their own relationship difficulties. It can feel frustrating to find exactly the right time, when you both are available, but it's worth any annoyance that scheduling causes. Do it when the entire family can be together.

After you deliver the news, your child will need some time and physical space, so avoid a school night or the last night of a vacation. A Saturday, after morning activities, or the beginning of a school break, even if just a couple of days, allows you and your ex to answer questions and help with the initial shock and emotional pain. It also gives your child time to sit with and process the information. Have no travel or other plans to be away after delivering the news. Many parents "hit and run," meaning that they tell their children and immediately escape reality by literally leaving home. Stay physically and emotionally present for your child even if it makes you feel uncomfortable.

Expect tears, anger, disbelief, denial, tantrums, and accusations—possibly all at once. If your child seems nonchalant or OK, don't be fooled. Children have exceptionally effective defenses that protect them from feeling hurt or vulnerable. Wait for an authentic emotional reaction. It will come. Maybe today, maybe tomorrow, maybe next week or next month—but it will come.

How to Tell Your Child

You created your family together, so you should undo it together. However you make the announcement, do it clearly and consistently, in a way that avoids misunderstanding or misinterpretation. Deliver it in the gentlest, most straightforward way that you can manage. That means making sure you and your soon-to-be-former partner are aligned in your message *before* you deliver the news, and remaining consistent when your child continues to ask "Why?" after that first conversation. Having one voice can bring some stability and comfort to the situation for your kid. The burden of remaining calm, amicable, and mature, of absorbing your child's distress without reacting, breaking down, becoming defensive, or acting out, lies with you and your ex. You both have a responsibility as parents to shoulder that burden.

In certain circumstances, you alone may have to deliver the news. Abandonment, substance abuse, or physical abuse may necessitate removing yourself and your child from harm's way before deciding to divorce. Safety always come first.

Whether you're telling your child together or solo, prepare answers to all their possible questions. For example:

"Why are you getting divorced?"
"Do you still love each other?"
"Did you ever love each other?"
"Am I going to have to move?"
"Will I have two houses? Where will I sleep?"
"Will I have to move schools?"
"Where will you/Mom live?"
"Will I be able to see you/Dad whenever I want?"
"How will we have [important holiday]?"
"Will [pet] come with me when I go to your house/Mom's house?"
"Are you going to get married again? Will I have stepparents or stepsiblings?"

Even if your child doesn't seem to understand what you're saying, expresses denial, or feels too upset to ask questions right away, questions will come, a lot of them, as the news sinks in. You don't need answers to every question right away. If you don't know yet, it's fine to say so, but don't ignore questions, and understand that you'll have to answer them all eventually, even if those answers cause pain or disappointment.

Children under age six believe that they stand at the center of the universe or the center of your universe. Unfortunately, this psychology means that, when something bad happens, kids often believe that they caused it. All kinds of fantasies, fears, and worries swirl around their heads. *Was it my fault? Did I make this happen because I was angry at you/Dad? If I was nicer/listened better/obeyed more, would you have stayed together?* This natural but mistaken logic makes it especially important that you reassure them. Nothing that they did, said, felt, or imagined prompted your decision. They are in no way responsible.

Kids commonly fear that, if their parents are splitting, they will leave them, too. Reassure your child that, sometimes, parents who loved each other when they married may fall out of love, but parents never stop loving their children. Explain that love between grownups may change, but parental love is unconditional and forever. You can say that it's normal for married people to disagree and even fight. It doesn't always lead to divorce, but when the fighting becomes constant, parents sometimes do better raising kids while living separately. Reassure them that you'll coparent them, both of you working hard to love them, take care of them, and change as little as possible. Even older children want to know that their parents cared for each other at some point. The myth of being born into love or from a loving match matters for foundational self-esteem. If that's not the case, it's a white lie worth telling.

How Much Information Is Too Much?

Your child will want to know why you're divorcing. After your initial conversation, they may want more details. Before the announcement, decide what to share and stick to that plan. Limits matter just as much as honesty. You and your ex still need privacy, so don't share the intimate details of your personal life. It's enough to say that you grew apart and no longer felt happy living together. Remain neutral. You can frame your answer in terms of different wants or needs. For younger kids you can say:

"Dad liked to stay home, and Mom liked to travel."
"Dad liked to work a lot, and I liked to spend a lot of time with the family."
"Mom liked going out with friends, and I liked quiet time at home."

If the question, "Didn't you know that about Dad when you married?" arises, answer that sometimes people change over the years. Some couples can adapt, and you tried hard but couldn't. Under no circumstances resort to name-calling or character assassination. Even if objectively true, saying, "Mom had an affair and doesn't love us anymore" or "Dad is lazy and mean to me, and I couldn't stand it anymore" hurts your child deeply. Remember that *you're* divorcing your ex, but your kid isn't. If a significant age disparity exists between or among your kids, have separate conversations with them and don't be surprised if older kids want to talk with you both, one-on-one.

I was treating a 14-year-old boy whose father told him that his mother had stopped having sex with him. No teenagers want to think about their parents having sex. Again, don't burden your kid. Oversharing can consist of saying too much about the details of your marital problems, but it also can come in the form of too much information about your internal conflicts. Anything that spills your own emotions or inappropriate information onto your child will cause confusion and distress. Work through your own conflicts and feelings with other supportive adults. If you don't have a great social support system, seek professional help.

If the divorce stems from infidelity or substance abuse, older children may have some awareness of the issue(s) already. Nevertheless, exclude any infidelity from your initial conversations. If your child asks directly about infidelity, answer as neutrally as possible. "When marriages break up, it's never about another person. It's about the problems between the two people in the marriage." If the main issue is substance abuse, you can say, "Your mother is ill but isn't getting help for her illness. Until that happens, we need to live apart to keep you safe."

It's OK to share normal feelings of sadness, anger, and disappointment with your kid, as long as you monitor the intensity and degree of those emotions. Never share rage, anxiety, depression, or intense feelings of loss or abandonment. All kids are emotional sponges, and they will absorb everything you share.

One of the hardest parts about divorce is that, as a parent, you're all in, 24/7, with all the unending busyness and chaos that comes with single parenting—or you're alone. If you're dealing with ongoing fears of being alone, loneliness, and loss, don't dump that on your child. Doing that will make them feel guilty. For this point, be especially careful with adolescents, who are separating from you as they form their own identity. Let your teen know that you'll be OK when they're away; that, while you prefer to be with them, you have friends, family, and a separate life that makes you happy when they're with your ex.

The Key to Good Communication

The saying goes that God gave each of us two ears and one mouth, so we're supposed to listen twice as much as we speak. But most people aren't good listeners. Listening means not just understanding spoken words; it also means reading body language and other nonverbal cues, as well as taking the temperature of the overall communication. As a parent, you already know that sensitivity and empathy will help you build a healthy relationship with your child. When you're divorcing, those two qualities become even more important.

Ask specific, open-ended questions. When you ask, "How was your weekend at Dad's?" or "What's Mom's new place like?" You likely will receive a curt, defensive one-word answer: "Fine." Asking more detailed or open-ended questions shows more interest and understanding, often resulting in more engaged responses. For instance, "Tell me about meeting your dad's new girlfriend this weekend. Did you get along with her? How did it go?" or "Did you get your new bed at your mother's this week? Tell me about the sheets you picked out."

Tone makes a big difference. Keep your questions curious rather than aggressive or intrusive. Also take cues from your child. If they don't want to share details from their time with the other parent, that's OK. *Not* having to share can feel liberating for some kids. Just make sure to let them know that you're open to talking at any time. Being receptive but not demanding leaves the door open for your child to share on their own terms.

If your child, whether age 6 or 16, appears upset after time away from you, use reflection to help them express their distress, specifically a technique called mentalizing.[1] Reflect what they may be feeling by putting their feelings into words and use your imagination to guess what may be making them feel sad, angry, or upset. For instance, "I could see that you were upset when you came back from Dad's. Do you want to talk about it?" "You seem a little sad and distant today. I wonder whether you feel upset because I didn't have time to talk after your weekend with Mom."

The phrase "I wonder" can work wonders as a conversation opener: "I wonder whether you missed [pet] this weekend." "I wonder if it was hard having to miss your baseball game to go to Dad's place." "I wonder..." not only reaches for deeper understanding, but it also leaves room for them to say "I'm not feeling that" and/or "I don't want to talk about it."

As parents, we naturally want to protect our children from all discomfort and pain, but that's not possible. Even if it were, it's also not healthy. We build resilience by dealing with discomfort, learning what negative feelings mean, and working through them. Telling kids that they shouldn't feel sad, angry, or uncomfortable, or making them feel bad about having those feelings is, about protecting yourself and trying to control a loss not in your control.

When talking to their kids about the other parent, adults sometimes fall into the trap of "me, too." You can be an empathetic listener, finding common understanding, without letting your own feelings toward your ex derail the conversation. If your child says "I hate Dad! I can't do anything right when I'm over there," responding, "OMG! I know. Dad is *so* mean and critical," reshapes the conversation around your feelings. Instead, you could say, "I understand that you feel sad when Dad criticizes you. Have you told him that?" This conversation validates your child's emotions and offers a way to create a better relationship with the other parent.

How we label things matters, especially in a divorce. What's mine versus yours, one parent versus the other's, can become an issue. Divide material belongings privately and don't involve your child in that process. Using neutral descriptions can help disarm the issue, too. Instead of Mom's house and Dad's apartment, you can say Main Street and Foster Avenue, or the green house and the apartment.

Custody of the family pet(s) can become as contentious as negotiating custody of the children. Young children identify family pets—yes, even the goldfish—as siblings. Older children and teens often do, too, especially if they grew up together. If you refer to the dog as Mom's dog, it is not such a stretch for younger children to feel like, if they're Dad's child, they can't be Mom's child, too. Avoid that pitfall by calling family pets by their own name.

It's OK to Say That You Don't Know

Children see their parents as all-powerful, all-knowing, and all-seeing until around age eight. It's important to maintain this illusion—the same as allowing them to believe in the Easter Bunny, Elf on the Shelf, Santa Claus, and the Tooth Fairy—because it protects them from stress and makes them feel safe and secure. When my husband was seven years old, he believed that, when his father was driving, he knew every road in the world. Not true of course, but the belief made my husband, as a boy, feel that nothing bad would happen when they were in the car.

But parents don't know everything, can't predict everything bad that will happen, and can't control everything. All children eventually must grapple with that reality, particularly those going through a divorce. Children asking questions that we can't answer are experiencing the difficulties of the adult world often for the first time. They realize that parents aren't perfect and all-powerful, that bad things *can* happen. When your child asks you a question, "I'm not sure" or "I don't know" is an appropriate and authentic response. If your child asks, "Am I going to Mom's this weekend?' and you don't know, answer honestly: "I don't know yet, but I'll try to find out. If you're not going to Mom's, we'll spend time together."

Promises Are Sacred

False promises can compromise your child's trust in you, so make promises carefully and only when you can fulfill them. Don't make promises for anyone else, including your ex. If your eight-year-old asks, "Can we visit Grandma in Florida this winter?" and you don't know whether you'll have the resources or your ex might change the custody schedule, don't automatically respond, "Of course, we can." Instead, say something like: "I think that sounds fun. I should know better in a few weeks, but I can't promise." Acknowledge their desire and your wish to make it happen while sharing that it might not be possible.

Parents often make promises that they can't keep because they want to feel loved, they feel guilty, or they can't bear their children's disappointment, sadness, or anger. The worst reason to promise your child anything is to avoid conflict. That and disappointment are a part of life, and divorces are full of both. Acknowledge any feelings of disappointment, yours and/or your child's, and work through them rather than lying to make yourself feel better.

Communicating with Your Ex

As long as you have children, you and your ex remain connected, even if you never want to see or speak to that person again. You'll have to discuss custody, holidays, vacation, college plans, wedding seating, and more. You probably loved and cared for your ex at some point. Dig deep to rememberIt can prove challenging to ask for changes to the custody schedule or express concerns about what happens when your child is with your ex. Those conversations can blow up in a thousand different ways. Thankfully, you can learn how to initiate change without starting a fire, which we'll review in the next section.

Whenever possible, to resolve differences, have conversations face to face or on the phone. Don't approach communication with hostility in your tone or words. ("This weekend is Mother's Day. I should have the kids! I can't believe you haven't bothered to think about that.") Instead, be clear and direct without being aggressive: "It's your weekend with Sam, I know, but Sunday is Mother's Day. Can we adjust the schedule so she's with me this weekend and you for the weekend of Father's Day?" If speaking directly to your ex causes too much pain or quickly becomes counterproductive, short, thoughtful, emotionally neutral emails offer a good way to make plans or suggestions, float changes to the schedule, and ask questions.

Texting offers little in the way of context, subtlety, or tone, making it one of the worst ways to communicate. Reserve anything other than scheduling questions or logistical issues—"Running 10 minutes late," "Please pack Terry's extra pair of pajamas for Sunday," or "What time is Chris's doctor's appointment tomorrow?"—for a different form of communication. *Never text when upset or angry.* No good will come of it.

If every conversation with or email to your ex hits a defensive, angry wall, consider engaging a parent coordinator. It's not cheap, but it's money well spent. A parent coordinator usually costs less than an attorney and has the professional qualifications and psychological attunement for what's best for children. Most parent coordinators don't see their role as one of a therapist, but many of them work as therapists, too, and can help diminish tension between parents, again, by focusing on what's best for the kids. It may be hard to find a parent coordinator who you both like and trust, but in difficult situations, it's worth the effort. It will save you both a lot of grief and conflict in the long run.

Positive Manipulation

Objectively speaking, manipulation is just a communication technique. As with any technique, anyone can use it in positive or negative ways. Guilting or coercing your child ("If you loved me, you'd want to spend [holiday] with me, not Dad.") hurts both your kid and the parent-child relationship. Incentivizing or encouraging your child ("It's bath time. Let's use the purple bubbles, and we'll read an extra book before bed") makes what could become a protracted struggle easier for you both.

These rules also apply to adults. It's OK to tell your ex that they did a great job as a parent in a certain situation. That kind of verbal support functions as positive manipulation. It's *not* OK to guilt your ex about having or not having the kids during the holidays. That tactic may work in the short run, but it will create problems in the future—especially if your ex flips the same tactics on you.

In some situations, you'll need to address potentially contentious issues, problems, or disagreements about how to raise children. If communication with your ex is less than amicable, and sometimes even if it's good, use the stroke-kick method of positive manipulation. Start with a compliment, words of support, or a reflection of what you perceive that your ex is feeling.

"Charlie loves coming to your apartment—"
"You're doing such a great job with Jamie at bedtime—"
"When we hand off the kids, I can see that you're upset—"

Then, add the criticism, suggestion, or request.

"—but often gets upset when you run late."
"—but the dark scares him. Maybe you could try to stay with him a bit longer."
"—Would it be better for me to wait in the car when I come to pick them up?"

Stroke-kick works nearly every time.

Don't Use Your Child as a Messenger

If you have something to say to your ex, say it to your ex. Asking Avery to tell your ex that, on Friday afternoon, you want to drop him off later or asking Parker to tell your ex that you don't want her boyfriend staying over isn't OK. Yes, it's challenging to communicate with a former partner, but keep the kids out of it. Don't burden them with conveying concerns, desires, or worries. Making them messengers creates an unnecessary emotional burden, and like the game of Telephone, it can distort the message. If they accidentally deliver an incorrect message, children will feel responsible and guilty. They already have enough worries of their own without absorbing yours. Along the same line, never ask your child to spy on your ex and report back to you. No good will come of that, either.

Technology Can Help

Video communication has changed the way that children can relate to a non-present parent. In terms of closeness or togetherness, the telephone never quite cut it. Seeing facial expressions, body language, and other nonverbal cues can bring families closer together and can help you to raise a more emotionally secure child. All methods of communication have limitations, though. Children under age three may have difficulty with technology, and they definitely have brief attention spans. Don't blame your ex for the limitations of technology with younger children. There's only so much anyone can do to keep a two-year-old focused on Facetime.

Let your child regulate the need for contact and remember that it goes both ways. If you give your kid the freedom to speak to the non-present parent, it's more likely that, when you're not present, your child will have easier access to you.

If You Just Can't

When every interaction with your ex, even the most benign or neutral, ends in conflict and acrimony, it's time to get help. Professional guidance can help you work through your anger or defensiveness and help you both focus on your child's needs. In some cases, a few sessions can do the trick; in others, a consistent schedule of weekly or bimonthly sessions can make coparenting run more smoothly. As we've discussed, parent coordination can help. Other options work, too, such as couple's therapy. Therapy is not just for trying to stay together! It can work wonders when couples are trying to coparent.

Children going through or who have been through a divorce should see a therapist at some point. Make parent guidance part of that therapy. A good child or adolescent therapist can see a child's issues in the family context, and good child therapists won't even see a child without also treating the parents. As a bonus, that kind of therapy can help you negotiate with your ex. But even if your ex won't agree to working with a parent coordinator or to seeing a couple's therapist, working by yourself with your child's therapist at least twice a month can help.

Lastly, again, see your own therapist. You can make major changes in your relationship with your ex by making changes in yourself, becoming more emotionally secure, more accepting of the loss, and more hopeful for the future.

4

LEGAL DECISIONS, EMOTIONAL CONSEQUENCES

When parents prioritize themselves above their children's emotional well-being, the proceedings of divorce can devastate kids. Legal decisions have profound emotional effects on parents and children alike, and a court's judgment of your child's best interests may not align with what truly benefits your kid's emotional health and security.

I'm not an attorney, but I have worked with hundreds of divorcing families. Your lawyer is your best source of legal advice, and every state has different laws governing divorce, financial support, and custody. This chapter will help you understand the emotional ramifications of your legal decisions. Divorce is hard enough for children when everything goes smoothly.

Mediation versus Litigation

When ending a marriage, the two most common routes are mediation or litigation.

In mediation—which is less confrontational, adversarial, expensive, and emotionally draining—a neutral legal professional (sometimes a lawyer) works with both spouses to come to a fair, equitable agreement on custody and financial issues. There are no witnesses, and the children don't take part in the proceedings. The mediator collects a flat or hourly fee, which is usually split equally between the divorcing parties, unless agreed otherwise. Depending on where you live, additional costs may apply for filing the divorce, evaluating property, and other expenses. Mediation saves time and money if you do some work on your own. Decide in advance where you can agree and bring those issues to the table with your mediator. Use them to help achieve compromises in areas of disagreement. In a perfect world, all divorces would be mediated—a tall order, I realize.

Litigation can cost eye-watering sums of money, with no guarantee of an outcome that you want or need. When fair settlement proves impossible—when one or both spouses are unstable and/or dangerous or a real risk of violence or abuse exists—litigation may become necessary. In litigation, attorneys become your avatars, like Rock 'Em Sock 'Em Robots, a toy where each player controls a robot to fight the other person's robot. Interview more than one attorney to ensure that you're choosing someone who best will represent you and your values, working toward a fair agreement between you and your ex that also supports your child's needs. This route costs more, but in certain situations, it's money well spent.

Litigating a divorce, a protracted process, often causes pain for kids. Because so many cases overwhelm and clog the system, judges can take *months* to make decisions—and that's after the wait just to get on the court docket. The rush to the finish line becomes a long, slow slog to the bottom. Even if judges and other adults try to make it easy on the children, there's no getting around the stressful process. Children may need to testify, in court or in a judge's chambers, about a parent or living situation. They may have to decide which parent they'd prefer to live with.

Litigation often involves forensic psychologists. Forensic psychologists can be therapists, but they don't play a therapeutic role. The court suggests or sometimes mandates them to evaluate the family psychologically: parents, children, caregivers, and perhaps even extended family. The psychologists' training flushes out any underlying mental health issues in parents, including physical or sexual abuse, neglect, or substance abuse. They often recommend or prescribe therapy or mental health treatment for children and parents in need of help. Unless an obvious danger threatens a child, their report contains observations rather than recommendations.

When parents can't agree on a custody agreement, a forensic psychologist can help. With a parent struggling to secure full custody because the ex's behavior could put the children at risk, the forensics process usually protects those vulnerable children from harm. It's not a pleasant process, however, because the forensic psychologist pries into every detail of your life, past and present, and the life of your child.

Most forensic psychologists and judges don't have sufficient education about attachment issues for children still being breastfed or who remain very attached to the primary caregiving parent. In the past two decades, courts have been taking fathers' and nonprimary parents' rights more seriously. That's good, but it ignores the real needs of children under age three, especially sensitive kids, or those who are attached to their mother or primary caregiver.[1]

Many forensic psychologists and judges still favor fifty-fifty custody agreements that treat children as material possessions to be split down the middle like muffins. Those officials are looking for a quick, uncomplicated solution, not one that involves nuance or considers individual family dynamics. It's often easier to focus on what's fair for the adults rather than on what children need, a perspective that this book aims to change.

The Power of Parent Coordination

Parent coordinators can help parents negotiate custody agreements and, once approved by a court, implement them. They assist parents in organizing the details and logistics of sharing children. Adept at parent guidance, coordinators act as a neutral third party to navigate disagreements about parenting styles, custody schedules, and difficult decisions that inevitably arise in divorce. Parents can use a coordinator voluntarily or, when they can't agree, a judge may mandate one. A coordinator removes the burden of parents having to deal with conflicts on their own. Appointments can take place weekly, monthly, or when a specific crisis or conflict occurs.

If parent coordination can't resolve major disagreements, parents often have to go back to court. While not the best outcome, it's sometimes necessary, particularly if the situation threatens the well-being of a child. Divorcing parents often find it hard to agree on anything, let alone major decisions about their children's health, education, and activities. Even parents who agree on financial issues and custody schedules often disagree about who should make those decisions. Parent coordinators often bring former partners to agreement, but in many cases, one parent fights for sole authority to make decisions even if sharing custody.

CASE STUDY

Take George and Alina, who had very different ideas about their son's and daughter's schooling and medical issues. The court suggested parent guidance, and I worked with them as a parent coordinator. The couple saw me weekly for one month, and it wasn't hard to see why they ended up in my office. George wanted the children to attend public school. Alina insisted on a private Waldorf school. George demanded that the children see a traditional pediatrician and receive all recommended vaccinations for childhood illnesses. Alina, concerned about the side effects of vaccination, wanted the children to see a naturopath and acquire immunity naturally. George believed in strict discipline, and Alina parented more gently and permissively.

In the first step of the process, each parent listened to the other's perspectives and concerns without interrupting. Stepping back, George could appreciate Alina's preference for the smaller classes and individual attention of private education,

> but he worried about the financial burden. Alina offered to cover the tuition, to which George agreed. Alina found a pediatrician to administer vaccines over a longer schedule, to which George also agreed as long as the children received all appropriate vaccines by age 2.

Even when living in an intact nuclear family, children adjust easily to different parenting styles. (For instance, which parent does your child approach when they want candy before dinner, or to watch TV instead of doing homework?) It is easier for children to accommodate different styles in different homes because they don't have to deal with the push-and-pull of conflicting demands.

Custody and Visitation Agreements

Frequently, parents seek equal time with their children without considering the children's emotional health and needs. That often makes custody agreements the most difficult part of a divorce to negotiate. First, let's acknowledge that fathers or nonprimary caregiving parents matter. Divorces should respect and provide for their rights and need to spend time with their children. Many studies demonstrate the importance of fathers in young children's lives.[2]

But—a very big but—with children under age three, especially those who are breastfeeding, or with older children who are extremely attached to their mother or primary attachment figure, what seems fair for parents can hurt the child. I will remind you that if you're going to prioritize your child's emotional well-being and mental health, you may need to set aside your own needs temporarily. It all has to do with attachment. So much misunderstanding surrounds this issue among divorce attorneys, judges, forensic psychologists, and even some parent coordinators who see young children as more resilient and capable of dealing with stress than they are. So, let's clarify again.

According to John Bowlby, the father of attachment theory, the primary attachment figure is the parent who spends the most time with a child throughout the day and who soothes them and helps regulate their emotions from moment to moment. In the past, that figure almost always was the mother. Today, fathers take on that role more often. In same-sex couples, one person often takes the role of primary parent. According to the World Health Organization, breastfeeding is still best for children under age two, both for immunological protection and for attachment security.[3]

From birth to age three is the first and most important critical period of brain development, primarily for the right brain, which regulates emotions and stress, among other activities.[4] It tells us when we are in danger, when we are out of danger and can relax, and enables us to read social cues. A child's secure attachment to the primary caregiver crucially enables right brain development and is essential for them to develop a sense of safety and security.[5] Trust and resilience to future stress starts here. When you separate a child under the age of three, particularly one who is breastfeeding, from their primary attachment figure, that child is at risk for attachment disorders and mental health instability later in life.[6]

Parents need to be honest and forthcoming about their parenting roles. When they can't, courts need to identify and agree on the primary attachment figure before deciding custody arrangements. In the acrimony of divorce, parents often lose sight of the difference between fairness for themselves and fairness for the children, and courts unfortunately don't do much to mitigate the situation.

As children grow older, and become more comfortable with separation and divorce, spending more time with the nonprimary parent, including overnights and weekday afternoons, becomes possible without causing harm. In time, children organically acclimate to parents' living separately—but *only* if the parents don't force self-centered change on them.

Unfortunately some of the most common custody arrangements, such as 2-3-2, 2-2-3, 3-4-4-3, and 2-2-5-5, move children around like they are a sack of potatoes. In the first formula, a child spends two days with one parent, three days with the other, and returns to the first parent for two days.

It's challenging for many adults, let alone their kids, to keep track of these overly complicated arrangements. In these situations, children move from home to home, constantly readjusting to a different household and different routines, while attending school and participating in extracurricular and other social activities.

Children do best with stability and routine. Young children, from birth to age three, should reside full-time with the primary attachment figure. Visitation with the other parent shouldn't include overnight visits until after weaning or until the child clearly feels comfortable being away from the primary figure for an extended period. Weaning too young, especially if breastfeeding, can harm children's emotional security when they need it most, such as during a divorce.

The best arrangement for children older than three is 5-2 or 4-3. They live with the primary parent during the school week, and the other parent gets either Saturday and Sunday, or Friday evening, Saturday, and Sunday. In this arrangement, a child doesn't have to deal with disruptive transitions while trying to focus on school. It also works best when one parent works full time and is more available on weekends. Like all custody arrangements, it comes with carefully considered compromises. One parent gives up the child during most work weeks, while the other gives up the child on most weekends.

In a 5-2 or 4-3 arrangement, children can have weekday time with the nonprimary parent after school, doing homework and having dinner, before returning to the primary home to sleep. As children get older, they usually can handle shorter stays in each parent's home and more of the back-and-forth and changes in routine. For a sensitive child, the least amount of transition works best. These children often resent disruptions more and blame one or both parents for having to change locations frequently.

CASE STUDY

Before their divorce, Derek stayed at home, and Emily worked at a consulting firm, putting in long hours and traveling for work several times a year. She mostly saw their son, Trevor, early in the morning and on weekends. With a mediator, Derek and Emily created a 2-3-3 custody schedule, but a year later, they were struggling with it. Trevor, age 5, was having a terrible time adjusting. He was throwing more tantrums, having trouble settling in the evenings, and often cried inconsolably over forgetting his favorite pajamas or his soccer ball, among other behavioral issues.

The custody schedule, while fair to the parents, didn't account for Trevor's strong attachment to his dad. When with his mother, he was often cared for by sitters. He loved his mother deeply, but before the divorce, his father had been caring for and comforting him every day.

Emily didn't want to give up time with Trevor, but she accepted that the mediated schedule wasn't working for him. She and Derek agreed that, for a year, Trevor would stay with his father, in what had been the family home, from Sunday night to Friday after school. Derek dropped Trevor at Emily's apartment on Friday night, and she returned him to his father on Sunday after lunch. Emily also arranged her work schedule to leave at five p.m. on Wednesdays. She and Trevor had dinner together on that night, and she returned him to his father in time for his bath and bedtime.

After a few weeks, Trevor had fewer tantrums; he resisted bedtime less and slept through the night more frequently. Derek and Emily agreed to revisit the schedule at the end of the year and to consider then whether to make changes to give Emily more time with Trevor in the future, as long as those changes worked for Trevor.

Adolescents are another story entirely. The closer kids are to adulthood, the more control they want and often need in their living situation. Developmentally, they're separating from parents and family to create their own identity.[7] Parents often give adolescents more control over coming and going because, in some cases, they'll take it even if it is not given. Not respecting a teenager's growing independence or reasonable requests, such as changing the custody schedule to stay closer to school before a big test or social commitment, can breed emotional distance and resentment.[8] Rigidly enforcing the rules of an agreement, without any flexibility, will push adolescents away. Listening to teenagers earns their respect and fosters closeness.

When Litigation Becomes Inevitable

If you can, avoid a protracted court battle over custody and resources. I know this is not always possible. If you need to go to court, keep as much of the conflict away from your child as you can. The impact of litigation on your kid depends more on how you and your ex handle the process than on the duration of the proceedings. In this situation, your child will pick up on some of the stress that you're feeling. Lying about how you're feeling isn't a good idea, but here's another place where containment matters. Save strong emotions for friends, family, or professionals. If your child is worrying about you, you can say honestly and reassuringly: "Yes, I'm a little stressed about going to court today, but I'm certain everything will work out."

If you have to deliver bad or disappointing news about a court decision that you know will upset your child, have the conversation with your ex present. However, if your ex is a contributing factor to the issue, you may need to deliver the news alone. In either situation, listen more than you talk, empathizing and reflecting your child's feelings as much as possible.

CASE STUDY

Mita and Amit divorced when their son, Tarak, was 7. Mita received primary custody. Amit saw his son every other weekend, spent two afternoons per week with him, and walked him to school on some mornings. By age 11, Tarak had become a talented soccer player, playing on a team that practiced four times a week after school at a venue half an hour from Mita's house and an hour from Amit's. Attendance was mandatory; the coach benched any player who missed a certain number of practices or games.

Amit disliked the travel involved in taking his son to practice and games, and waiting for them to end. He told Mita and his son that the travel, practices, and games interfered with this quality time with Tarak and that he wouldn't take him to practice or games on his custody days. That decision understandably upset Tarak. Mita asked her lawyer to petition the court to compel Amit to take their son to practice and games. The judge refused, agreeing that it interfered with the father's time with his son.

The news infuriated Mita, but she processed her feelings before telling Tarak. That night, after dinner, she asked him to shut off the TV so they could talk.

"I know what I'm about to tell you is going to be disappointing, and I know you're going to have a lot of feelings about it," she began. "The judge decided that your dad doesn't have to take you to practice or games. I'm so sorry. I know how important it is to you."

She waited for him to say something, but he remained silent.

"Do you want to talk about it?" she asked.

Tarak started to cry. "He's so selfish! I hate him! I never want to see him again! What about what I want?"

Mita took a deep breath. "I hear how angry you are, and

you have a right to be angry. But not seeing your father isn't an option because this was a legal decision. There's nothing I can do right now, but you can tell your father how you feel. Maybe he'll change his mind. If he doesn't, we can talk to the coach, explain the situation, and ask if they can make an exception. If that's not possible, we can look for a more flexible team that you can join."

Mita reflected her son's feelings without disparaging his father and gave Tarak permission to speak directly to Amit about how the decision affected him. She didn't make promises that she couldn't keep, and she offered to help her son explore other options.

Unfortunately, neither Mita's explanations nor Tarak's pleas changed Amit's decision. Although sympathetic to Tarak, the coach couldn't make an exception for him. Amit insisted on maintaining the court-ordered custody schedule, but Tarak didn't speak to or voluntarily visit his father for months. Eventually Mita found a more accommodating team for Tarak. But Tarak never forgave his father.

When it comes to school, social, or extracurricular activities, putting your own desires or needs before your child's rarely ends well. Sometimes, parents must prioritize themselves of course: when ill or when work that supports the family is at risk. But choose carefully where you take a stand, because your decision may have long-term consequences.

Preparing Your Child

Judges, lawyers, forensic psychologists, or social workers may ask children to speak about their feelings, custody preferences, and other issues. Children often do have preferences but resist sharing them with adults, for fear that they'll hurt one parent or the other or damage their relationship with both. Conflicting loyalties puts them in a terrible bind. The resulting stress can create anxiety, cause nightmares, and contribute to feelings of depression.

If your child must speak with the judge or any other professional in the process, let them know a few days beforehand. Sooner than that means sitting with anxious feelings for too long, but you also don't want to spring the announcement at the last minute. Listen to your kid's concerns about what will or might happen without adding your own comments. Mirror their feelings without judgment or criticism. For example:

> "I know you have to speak with the judge tomorrow. I can see that you're feeling stressed."
>
> "I imagine that it's hard to talk to the social worker about your dad and me. Do you want to share any of your thoughts or feelings about it?"
>
> "Whatever you say to the judge/social worker/psychologist is OK. It's important to tell the truth. We/I love you and support you no matter what the judge decides."

Explain that the court wants what's best for them. They should speak honestly and express their preferences clearly. Take away the burden that they have to get it right or say the right thing. Emphasize that nothing they can say will harm you, the other parent, or their relationship with either of you. *Don't* encourage them to lie or warn them that their opinions could harm their chances of staying with you or your ex. Doing that will create feelings of conflict, guilt, and confusion.

How to Create a Custody Plan That Puts Your Child's Needs First

Do:
- Take the age and emotional needs of your child into consideration when approaching custody and the legal process.

- Establish a flexible arrangement that sets rules but leaves room for compromise and adaptability.
- Turn to mediation as your first choice.
- Consider the long-term impact and consequences of your words and behavior on your child.
- Keep your child out of the legal process as much as possible.
- Dig deep to become your best, most secure self.

Don't:
- Involve your children in the mediation or legal process unless absolutely necessary.
- Discourage your child from telling the truth to other supportive adults.
- Punish your child for your ex's actions or neglect.
- Overshare about the divorce or your ex with your child.
- Use their fear of losing you or your love to threaten your child into speaking on your behalf.
- Use the custody agreement to feel powerful or in control if you feel out of control.
- Bring your own pain or feelings of rejection into negotiating a custody arrangement.
- Bribe your child with material objects or experiences to choose you.
- Make your child feel guilty about their feelings or preferences.

Divorce is a marathon, not a sprint. I know you want to get it over with quickly, but it will proceed at its own pace and in parallel to the rest of your life. Try not to let it take over the everyday routines and joys in your life, or your child's.

5

WHAT TO EXPECT FROM YOUR KID

No matter how you slice it, divorce is traumatic for children of all ages. No kid will pass unscathed through even the most amicable divorce, and it's unrealistic to expect that your kids will behave as though nothing happened. The children of parents who stick their heads in the sand, proceeding with business as usual, often have the hardest time. Your reactions to your kid's emotions and behaviors can make the difference between emotional resilience and fragility. Realistic expectations can help you cope with whatever comes your way. Here's what to expect.

Stages of Mourning

For many adults, the concept that children grieve seems unfathomable. But, of course, children mourn deeply when loved ones (including pets) die or when they feel neglected, misunderstood, or abandoned.[1] Losing a nuclear family can feel just like a death to a child.[2] Let's use Elisabeth Kübler-Ross's stages of grief[3] as a road map to understand the profundity of that loss and some of the feelings that children will face. These feelings don't necessarily occur in this sequence, nor do they necessarily take place only once.

DENIAL defends against emotional pain. Repression and denial, both unconscious defenses, would be great if they lasted forever. Denial can take many forms. At first, children may seem unbothered by news of their parents' divorce. They may say, "I don't want to talk about it," "I'm glad you finally decided to get a divorce," or even "Great! More toys for me!" Reality hasn't hit yet. Like a bandage over a serious wound, denial serves as only a temporary fix. At some point sooner or later, the wound will open.

ANGER is a normal, necessary response for anyone going through a divorce. The end of your marriage may feel like a relief for you, but for a child, it betrays an unspoken promise of permanence and stability, a disruption in their sense of security and a wound to their belief that they are your priority and the center of the universe. Even adolescents and young adults, who understand that parents are fallible, often feel this way.

Your child may direct anger at you, your ex, or both of you at the same time. That anger won't undo your relationship with your child, but how you handle it can. Listening without making excuses, empathizing, and accepting their feelings without defensiveness will soothe their distress and defuse their anger. Getting angry in response or, worse, ignoring or disregarding their feelings can lead to retaliation that escalates the conflict into yelling, name calling, breaking things, physical violence, or running away. Or a child might withdraw and internalize that anger, resulting in behavioral issues, depression, or anxiety.

BARGAINING is a way that children try to exercise control in a situation where they are essentially powerless. Younger children believe that everything revolves around them. They think that they have the power to influence reality, which of course they don't. In this kind of magical thinking—"If I do X, then Y will happen"—they often assume personal responsibility or blame for the divorce. Younger children commonly say, "If I'm good/do better in school/listen more, will you stay together?" Adolescents often apologize: "I'm sorry I've been such a pain. If you stay together, I'll stay out of trouble." Even older, more emotionally sophisticated children may feel guilty, wondering whether they contributed to parental disagreements or whether they could have done something different to avert their parents' split. Parents frequently struggle with this stage because they must confront their children's unhappiness head on.

SADNESS   is to be expected. The loss of the family ideal—even if reality looked less than ideal—makes for a deeply sad experience for children. For them, an imperfect nest is still a nest.

ACCEPTANCE   is grief's ultimate destination, but you can't rush it. It takes months or, in some cases, years. Some children never get there. But with acceptance come hope and resilience.

What Does Development Have to Do with It?

Depending on the age and cognitive and emotional development of your child, they will have different feelings and reactions to your divorce.[4] Toddlers experience the loss differently than do school-age children, who experience it differently than adolescents. You need to anticipate what your child is experiencing and know when it's time to bring in professional help.

Infants (birth–18 months)

If you think that infants and babies don't know what's happening around them, think again. They have an exquisite sensitivity to their environment, absorbing it and reflecting it back to their caregivers.[5] Infants experience the world physically: orally, by putting everything in their mouths, through sound, and through touch. They also see body language, facial expressions, signs of physical warmth, and affection. They understand the threat of loud, aggressive speech, and soft and soothing tones calm them. They respond differently when not touched, touched with tenderness, or handled harshly.[6] Every sensory experience is registered in their brain and adds to their rapid and expansive neurological growth.[7]

If you divorce before your child turns three, you need a deep understanding of their emotional needs and well-being. What happens during this period can make or break their future mental health. It bears repeating that children under age three need their primary attachment figure to remain physically and emotionally present and calm as much as possible to provide security and a feeling of safety.[8] If parents divorce before their children are three, the primary attachment figure should have primary guardianship. If that's not you, treating your child as a possession to obtain or win, or insisting on fifty-fifty shared custody, including overnight visits, will cause your child to suffer now and in the future. Never wean a breastfeeding child only because the other parent wants that. Weaning should happen organically, as if no divorce had taken place.

Most children naturally experience separation anxiety from around 8 to 18 months.[9] This developmental phase occurs when a baby realizes that the primary attachment figure can go away and not come back. It rocks their world, causing fear and anxiety. Separating a baby from the center of their universe amplifies that anxiety exponentially and can have lasting emotional consequences.[10]

Signs of infant stress include hitting or biting you, your ex, other family, babysitters, friends, and even pets. This aggression embodies the fight part of the fight-or-flight evolutionary response to danger. Signs of flight in a child include manic behavior, an inability to make eye contact, or rejecting a previously enjoyed activity. The child may cry more, experience more emotional volatility, have problems sleeping, resist physical affection, push away, and cycle among aggression, clinginess, and avoidance.[11] These behaviors can look like ADHD, but in the absence of that diagnosis and in the presence of a divorce, they point to stress. They also may be signs of the beginning of an attachment disorder, which can lead to mental health conditions later.

Toddlers (18 months–3 years)

These little ones have big feelings that they can't control or regulate on their own.[12] Even the most easy-going toddler in a stable family with understanding parents will feel overwhelmed and have meltdowns sometimes. As emotional sponges, toddlers absorb and express their parents' agitation, anger, sadness, and stress. We associate tantrums with toddlers for a reason.[13]

Tantrums

Toddler tantrums are the result of a blown emotional fuse. They often result from decisions or limitations imposed on the child, and the decision itself rarely matters: leaving the playground, taking a bath, receiving the wrong banana—meltdown. Divorce imposes even more frustrations on toddlers by short-circuiting their psyche: being with you when they want to be with the other parent, sleeping in an unfamiliar bed, not having their security blanket, pillow, or stuffy because someone forgot to put it in the bag. Thankfully, most kids outgrow throwing tantrums.

When your child is having a tantrum, stay present physically and emotionally. Don't leave, judge, punish, shame, or get angry. The tantrum will pass. If and when they let you, hug or hold them. When they calm down, put into words what they may be feeling. If your toddler doesn't want to come with you on a custody day, for example, you could say: "I can see that it feels hard to leave Dad today. Let's play in the backyard until you're ready to go."

Sleep

Trouble falling or staying asleep also may signal that toddlers are feeling the stress of divorce.[14] They may wake earlier in the morning, wake in the night and call for you, or want to come into your bed more than usual. They may have more nightmares or experience night terrors. In night terrors, which occur during non-REM sleep, the child partly wakes in a terrified state. Once awake, older children and adults recognize that dreams and images in night terrors aren't real. But that doesn't happen for toddlers. For them, the line between imagination and reality is much thinner, and fantasy often has the same power as real life. If your child has a nightmare or night terror, stay with them until they calm down, reassuring them that dreams feel real but aren't.

When your kid's sleep issues interrupt your own sleep, it might make you feel irritable or angry. As hard as it may feel, respond to your child's sleep problems with patience and understanding. Falling asleep and waking are transitional times, meaning that children feel more vulnerable then, so your kid needs you more at these times. Physical affection, including skin-to-skin contact, can help them feel safe. Avoid strict discipline around changes in sleep. Allow yourself to break the usual rules around bedtime or waking. You may decide to let your child sleep with you or to sleep in their room, to help them feel more secure. If those possibilities concern you, remember that it's not a permanent situation. When your child experiences sleep changes, the more sensitively and supportively that you respond, the more quickly the problem will resolve.

CASE STUDY

June and Sofia had been together for 10 years and had two children: Dallas, age 4, and Serena, age 2. June had an affair with another woman. When Sofia learned that June had been unfaithful, she told her wife to leave and filed for divorce. June moved into an apartment with her new girlfriend, and the children remained with Sofia. The divorce proceedings went relatively smoothly. June agreed not to contest Sofia's request for sole custody as long as she had visitation rights.

But even after the proceedings ended, Sofia remained furious at June, unable to shake her sadness about the failure of the marriage. She also had serious concerns about their kids. Dallas's school reported that, on several occasions, he had hit or bitten other children. Serena, previously a good sleeper, was having a harder time falling asleep, and Sofia had to spend more and more time with her at bedtime. Serena often woke in the night, seeking reassurance and comfort, and had nightmares. She told Sofia that she was afraid that her mothers would leave and not come back. She had been weaned, but she demanded to be nursed back to sleep.

Both women came to me for help. I recommended that Dallas see a child therapist and that June spend more time with both kids. I also urged Sofia to see her own therapist as a safe place in which to express her anger and sadness. Sofia brought Serena to some of our sessions so I could model how to calm and reassure her when she woke in the night. As a result of all that work, Serena felt secure again and returned to sleeping soundly. Dallas also responded positively, and his aggressive episodes at school tapered off.

Eating

Food nourishes the body, but eating also demonstrates control. Toddlers who throw food on the floor are declaring their independence. Don't be surprised if divorce changes your child's eating habits.[15] A toddler may become pickier, eat more or less than usual, or even stop altogether. In divorces, eating can become a power struggle between parents and children.

As with sleep changes, remain flexible. If you can exercise patience and do not fuss over what and how your child is eating, these new behaviors probably will pass. Acknowledge that, sometimes when feeling upset, eating is hard. Remind them that, when they feel hungry, they should eat. Don't force your child to eat unless a loss of appetite lasts for two weeks and significant weight loss occurs. In that case, bring them to their pediatrician *and* ask for a referral to a play therapist.

Aggression

Toddlers may become more aggressive—screaming, yelling, biting, hitting—which, if we're honest, we adults would like to do if we could get away with it. Stay calm; mirror their anger, sadness, and frustration with your body language; and put into words what you believe is happening. Those actions make children feel understood. More-verbal children usually behave less aggressive physically. For a child who is less verbal, a feelings chart, which has pictures of facial expressions with matching labels, offers a useful tool for identifying and naming emotions. Buy one, download one for free, or make your own. If you name what you see that they're feeling, they'll learn to use words instead of aggression to express themselves: "I understand that you're upset that you have to go to Mom's house today. You can tell me that you're upset, but you can't hit your brother. You can hit a pillow, or we can use your finger paints or markers to make an angry picture."

If you need to help your child with emotional regulation, try physical affection first. If that doesn't work, dancing to music, making art, roughhousing (pillow fight, inflatable punching toy), or sports all offer safe outlets for emotions and feelings.

Regression

During the divorce and for some time after, toddlers may regress, as happened with Serena.[16] A weaned child may want to breastfeed or take a bottle again. A potty-trained child may wet the bed again or want to wear diapers. They may make baby sounds instead of using words or want you to hold or carry them like babies. Don't worry about going with it temporarily. Accepting this regressive behavior reassures your child that they can connect with you as they did as an infant. If you go with the flow for a bit, they most likely will grow out of it. If the behavior continues, again, find a play-based therapist.

School-Age Children (3–8 years)

In this relatively tranquil period of development, children have more emotional stability, building self-esteem through understanding their strengths and weaknesses and building competencies in learning and other activities. At this age, children generally have an easier time handling changes. An emotionally sensitive child will need additional support. These are the years when learning issues typically arise, and impulsivity can peak. School-age children experience many of the same symptoms as younger children, including sleep issues, nightmares, aggression, and regression.

In this phase, children more likely handle divorce stress with a fight-or-flight response.[17] For example, an eight-year-old may get into fights at school or become distractible and show attention issues (flight). Emotional regulation—which is a learned behavior—consists of recognizing and controlling emotions.[18] School-age children have the language to describe what they're feeling, but they may struggle with expressing it. A feelings chart can prove just as useful for school kids as for younger ones, especially if the child is neurodivergent or has learning differences. Children of this age have more emotional control, but the disruption of divorce makes them more unpredictable. They may overreact to minor frustrations or have dramatic mood swings.

Asking these children why they were mean to a sibling or why they didn't do their homework doesn't work, because *they* usually don't know why. A nine-year-old working on a puzzle may sweep all the pieces to the floor. A six-year-old may hurl a box of crayons because the drawing isn't right. Getting angry and ordering them to pick everything up won't address the underlying problem. Help your child identify what they're feeling and why. For example: "I can see that you're frustrated. I wonder if you're feeling sad or angry. It's OK to feel that way and say, 'I'm sad because . . .' or 'I'm angry because . . .' Sometimes, doing that can make you feel better. You always can tell me how you're feeling, and I'll listen to you."

Divorces make it harder for children to tolerate frustration, and they may cope through increased impulsivity.[19] They may have less bandwidth for overstuffed schedules and overstimulation, less ability to handle academic pressure and after-school activities. Let them have more time for unstructured play, outdoor time, physical play, or downtime with you and their friends. Be flexible and check in with your child often. If your kid says, "I'm tired. Can I skip my lesson/practice today?" Don't immediately say, "No, you made a commitment." As with adults, sometimes activities can distract them from their troubles, and sometimes they just need to go home and sit on the couch with a bowl of popcorn. A break once in a while is fine. Continuing to blow off activities that they used to enjoy may indicate feelings of depression or shame about the family drama. But their interests also could be shifting, so don't assume depression. If other signs of depression, such as social isolation, mood swings, and sleep issues present themselves, go to a child therapist sooner than later.

Meet with your child's teachers *and* the school counselor to let them know about your family situation. This helps create a support system for your kid academically, socially, and emotionally. Sharing information about your child's reactions to the divorce and any concerns that you have will help the school contextualize new or problematic behavior. In the long run, your child likely will receive more positive attention and understanding overall.

CASE STUDY

Craig worked in finance, traveling constantly for work, and Pam worked as a management consultant for a major firm. Neither spent much time with their son, Damien, though Pam usually came home at seven p.m. to put him to sleep, and stayed a little later in the morning to send him to school with his loving nanny, who primarily raised him. Even before Pam and Craig told Damien that they were divorcing, they had difficulty coping with his behavior. He was often sullen and moody at home and rarely wanted to talk to them. His preschool called them in to discuss his behavior. As he grew older, his conduct didn't improve. At age 6, he often lost his temper during recess and, when frustrated, sometimes pushed other children.

Pam and Craig had been married for eight years when they decided to divorce. After Craig moved out, Damien's behavior deteriorated so much that the principal told Pam that the boy needed to see a therapist *and* start taking medication. That's when Pam and Craig came to me. They couldn't see it at first, but their son's impulsivity and aggression clearly resulted from his lack of contact with them. Their divorce offered an opportunity to improve their parenting skills, which they did.

Pam walked Damien to school and came home by five p.m. to spend bath time and bedtime with him. Craig collected him from school and spent several afternoons during the week playing with him. The boy stayed with his dad for three weekends per month.

Damien began seeing a play therapist, but to avoid embarrassment, his parents hadn't told the school about the divorce. I urged them to do so because, if the school knew what was happening, it could become an important ally. Reluctantly, Pam and Craig met with the principal, Damien's teacher, and the school counselor, and told them about the divorce, play therapy, and their reluctance about medicating their son. All parties agreed to touch base regularly, and the school suggested that, when Damien became disruptive in class or on the playground, a teacher would take him to a quiet room and spend some time with him alone until he regained control of his emotions. Damien also brought a comfort object to school, a piece of blanket that he could touch when feeling angry or overwhelmed.

Pam and Craig's divorce prompted them to align their

> priorities in a way that they hadn't done while married. They reoriented to Damien's emotional needs and partnered with the school. As a direct result, their son's behavior improved dramatically. By the end of the school year, he no longer needed his comfort object and rarely needed to use the quiet room.

Adolescents (9–25 years)

Even in stable environments, adolescence can prove stressful for kids *and* parents.[20] This second critical period of brain development is defined by dramatic physical change and emotional volatility. In the right, or social emotional part of the brain, the ventral striatum governs risk-taking, and the amygdala processes stress. Those two areas race ahead in development while the prefrontal cortex (PFC)—which regulates emotions, making decisions, and controlling impulses —doesn't develop fully until age 25 or sometimes later, especially in young men.[21] So, until the PFC catches up with the rest of the brain, teens and young adults struggle with impulse control, poor judgment, lack of perspective, self-consciousness, and self-criticism.[22] All this is happening while they're trying to navigate the physical changes of puberty, increased responsibilities at home and school, and the new social pressures of their peer groups. (The turbulence of your own teenage years makes so much more sense now, doesn't it?)

Like younger children, adolescents commonly go into fight-or-flight mode because of a divorce.[23] That response may make them more irritable and contentious at home and school. They may withdraw or isolate from family or peers. Distractibility or feelings of depression may cause them to struggle with schoolwork. The key is to help them put the pieces of the emotional puzzle together whenever they let you. If you see that they feel sad, angry, or distracted, don't try to cheer them or expect them to accept the divorce before they feel ready. Acknowledge their feelings and validate them. This will help them move along in the mourning process much more quickly than if you ignore their distress or push them to get to the finish line too quickly.

Be there when the door opens—literally. If you're not home when they come out of their room to get a snack or take a break, you may miss an opportunity for them to share how they're feeling. If you knock on their door, you may hear, "I'm busy," "Not now," or "Leave me alone," which you should respect. Don't barge in. During transitional times—waking up, having breakfast, going to school, coming home from school, going to bed—be present physically and emotionally. Again, as with younger kids, adolescents often feel most vulnerable and therefore more likely to communicate at these junctures. If you can, pick them up from school or activities, be home when they come home from school or socializing, and take them out for their favorite dessert.

For good, open communication, eye contact matters, but adolescents are trying to separate from parents to become their own person, so they often have a harder time with face-to-face conversation. So pivot—literally. Walking the dog, strolling in the park, or going for a car ride together all offer great opportunities for side-by-side communication.

As you did at their age, adolescents experience their emotions and feelings more intensely than their parents, including the anger, defiance, rebellion, resentment, sadness, and despair accompanying a divorce. Don't disregard, dismiss, or ignore your child's feelings and reactions as overly dramatic, overblown, or unimportant. Your sincere interest in their feelings, your ability to listen without reacting negatively or judging, and your empathy will help them metabolize their feelings. But again, if normal reactions to divorce last more than two weeks, seek professional help for your child and yourself.

6

BEING YOUR BEST SELF AS A PARENT

It's challenging to be your best self when you're going through a divorce. It's even more difficult to be your best parental self. We often talk about children regressing under stress, but let's face it: Adults do, too. Remember that you're divorcing your ex; your child isn't. Your pain matters, but it can't become your kid's pain.

When you feel any kind of pain—physical or emotional—caring for another person is difficult. You may want to curl into a ball and lick your wounds, but being a parent means not always having that option. Caring for yourself helps you care for your child. You need to make sense of what you're feeling and learn to deal with it in a healthy way. If you don't do that for yourself, you won't be able to do it for your child, either.

Self-Care and Support

It's been repeated so often that it's become a cliché: You have to put on your own oxygen mask before you can help someone else put on theirs. This is especially true in the case of divorce. If you don't care for yourself, you can't care for your child. Self-care can mean anything from finding time for exercise, therapy, or meditation, to sleeping well, eating right, and spending time with friends.

Time is the rarest commodity. No matter how much money we have or how good we are, we all have, as the song from *Rent* goes, 525,600 minutes a year. This means what you choose to do with that time matters in terms of being your best self. I sometimes forget my own advice and schedule so many patients that I don't have time to eat lunch or go to the gym. That makes me grumpy and less patient with patients and family. When that happens, I have to create boundaries that allow me to care for myself and restore my bandwidth to care for others.

Divorcing or divorced parents have lots of competing demands: caring for the kids, dealing with custody schedules, work, maintaining a home without a partner, and navigating a new kind of relationship with their ex. Often they think of caring for themselves last, which is short sighted. If you get sick or break down emotionally, your children will be lost.

Stress from divorce affects mind and body.[1] It also can trigger, you guessed it, fight-or-flight mode.[2] Increased levels of cortisol can dull your appetite, so you might forget to eat or don't eat enough.[3] When you do eat, you might binge because you don't know when you're going to eat again.[4] Anxiety and hypervigilance disrupt sleep.[5] You may not exercise or even want to move, in case you need energy to fight later. If you turned to a glass (or more) of wine or smoked a joint each night to relax, it may lose its power. Now it affects your sleep, makes you feel tired and depressed, and those extra calories from alcohol, a lack of exercise, or having the munchies have put on some extra pounds.

So how can you counter some of these stress responses and manage the excess cortisol in your system? One of the best things to counter the physical symptoms of stress is another physical experience. Exercise releases endorphins, a.k.a. happy hormones, and reregulates the metabolism and emotions.[6]

Sleep functions as a reliable barometer of emotional and physical well-being. If you're having trouble falling asleep, struggling to stay asleep, or are sleeping too much, there's a very good chance you are feeling stressed, anxious, or depressed.[7] Boringly regular sleep routines matter enormously for sleep hygiene. Establish a consistent bedtime and waking time—yes, even on weekends. At least an hour before bed, stop using your phone or computer or watching TV. Calming rituals—a warm bath, soothing music, journaling, affirmations, or prayer—also can help. Sleep experts recommend making your room as dark as possible and, if outside noise is an issue, using a white-noise machine.[8] Don't leave your phone or tablet where you can reach it if you wake in the night. Place it well beyond reach and, if you can, turn it off (which is better for battery life, anyway).

Meditation or behavioral relaxation work can help with anxiety and stress.[9] You don't need to have a formal practice or follow a particular teacher. Meditation can fit into the busiest day because as little as 10 minutes, twice per day, can have a positive effect. A 10-minute session can feel like an hour-long nap. Relaxation work slows your breathing, regulates your heartbeat, and increases circulation. Clients who have incorporated these practices into their lives tell me that it has increased their patience, optimism, and energy.

Intentional eating can help with stress management, too.[10] Fresh unprocessed foods, sufficient protein, and drinking lots of water will give your body good fuel to function. Sugar provides a burst of energy, but it burns quickly, exhausting your adrenal and immune systems. That quick jolt nosedives into a crash, followed by a long, slow slog uphill.[11] At least once a day, find time to sit down and enjoy your food. When you eat on the fly, you deny yourself the pleasure of eating, and pleasure offsets stress.

Socializing with friends also counts as self-care, and friends qualify as more than a support system. When you're going through a divorce, time with them isn't a frivolous luxury but a necessity. It reminds you that life goes on, refocusing you on happier, more fulfilling relationships.

In a divorce, friends will take sides. Some may choose you, and you may lose some to your ex. Most of the time, each partner keeps the friends that they brought to the relationship, but not always. Some of my patients remained friends with their ex's best friend. It's unusual, but it happens! You'll never regret time spent with good friends, but you may regret the isolation of removing yourself from their company.

Self-Awareness

Self-awareness is the key to being your best self. That's true in any situation, but during the emotional turmoil of a divorce, it can prove challenging to remember. Self-awareness means not only the recognition of your anger at your ex but also of your hurt, sadness, disappointment, and feelings of rejection and abandonment. It doesn't matter whether you left or your ex ended the marriage. In the end, you both are alone now.

Feelings of loss and hurt often open old wounds from the past. If you lost a parent as a child, or if your own parents divorced, or if you lost a friend, sibling, or loved one, that pain can become indistinguishable from the pain you're feeling now. If you struggled with self-esteem before your marriage and never resolved it, the divorce can knock down all the defenses around old hurts that never healed. Any unresolved traumas, including the emotional pain of past losses, can come back to haunt you and, by extension, your child. A lack of awareness regarding your own history and emotions may cause you inadvertently to repeat behaviors from your own childhood or to act out old dramas with your ex or child.

CASE STUDY

When they married, Jace loved Sara's sense of humor and her fiery, adventurous personality. An IT supervisor, he was a calm, self-contained planner. Sara was his opposite: a spontaneous, sometimes volatile artist, a risk-taker with passionate opinions. Before they married, Jace knew about Sara's turbulent family history. Her mother suffered from borderline personality disorder, and her father was an alcoholic. Her parents divorced when she was eight. Sara's mother had full custody, but she was verbally abusive, cold, and critical. In college, Sara developed an eating disorder and saw a therapist briefly, but she stopped going when she stopped binging and purging.

The couple had three children: Carter, Hope, and Franklin. When Franklin turned two, Sara started losing her temper more often, blowing up at the kids for small annoyances. When Jace intervened, she turned her anger on him and stormed out of the house for hours. She promised to control her outbursts but couldn't. It became clear that she was drinking heavily, and the last straw came when Jace discovered Franklin playing with a cache of empty mini vodka bottles in a corner of the pantry. The boy had opened one to taste it. When Jace confronted Sara, she exploded, telling him that she never loved him and wanted a divorce.

Jace sued for full custody and won. Because of her own alcohol abuse and emotional outbursts, Sara had supervised visitation. She agreed to go to rehab and went back to therapy, where she recognized that she was repeating her own family trauma. She spent as much time with her children as the court allowed and practiced what she learned in treatment about emotional regulation and stress management. At first, the kids hesitated to engage with their mother, but over time they learned to trust her again. When Jace saw that she was taking recovery seriously and earning his trust and the children's, he gave her more supervised time with them.

Anger Is Normal

You may be surprised to know that anger is a better motivator than sadness and hopelessness for moving forward and healing. In psychology, we call anger an activating emotion, meaning that it can move us to action that creates change.[12] When experiencing any loss, feeling angry is normal, but it's possible to get stuck there. If you can't get past your anger, you can't move on. Accepting the end of your relationship and that you have agency, self-determination, and (some) control will allow you to reclaim your life with the potential for love and happiness in the future. Moving past blame and anger models resilience, self-awareness, and self-respect for your children. It is also a far better place to be psychologically moving forward and essential if you are going to be able to be your best self as a parent.

You may have every reason to feel angry at your ex, and demonizing them may feel good in the short term. But holding that feeling and blocking or interfering with the relationship between your child and ex has very real consequences for you, for your relationship with them, and more important, for your children. As a result, your child may lose a beloved parent, turn against you for interfering, or both. Either way, it's a lose-lose situation, and many parents don't realize that they're doing it. If you badmouth your ex, hoping to create a rift between them and your child, it may in fact create a rift between *you* and your child. You can be sure your child will say something to your ex, setting up a war of words and possible retaliation. You are creating conflict rather than alleviating it.

CASE STUDY

When he was 12 years old, Philip's mother left his father and him. For Philip, the worst part of the divorce was his father constantly putting down his mother for her "money grabbing" and "selfishness." His father called her "irresponsible" and told Philip that "not even animals abandon their young." He ignored his son's pleas to stop.

Philip understood his father's anger, though, and felt angry, too. Even so, he couldn't express those feelings to his father,

> who never moved past his anger at his ex-wife. Philip also felt the need to defend his mother to balance the scales, even though his father had full custody.
>
> Later in life, Philip learned that, for years, his father had refused his mother's attempts to see her son, intercepting any correspondence from her and actively discouraging Philip from contacting her. (This is classic *parental alienation*.) Philip's damaged feelings toward his mother made him feel confused about whether he wanted to know her.
>
> As Philip got older, he distanced himself from his dad to deal with those conflicted feelings. In therapy with me, he came to forgive his mother, reaching out her to repair and rebuild their relationship. He eventually forgave his father, but their relationship never recovered completely.

If, after your divorce, you want your child to feel happy, healthy, resilient, and secure, you need to control your anger and present a neutral, if not caring, stance toward your ex. Exposure to your rage eventually will make it difficult for your child to feel love and loyalty to either of you.

This doesn't mean that, if your child tells you that they're angry at or upset with your ex, you have to tell them that they can't be. Honesty about your ex's behavior or decisions that affect your child doesn't mean that you have to make excuses. Don't jump on the bandwagon and pivot the conversation to yourself: "I know what you mean! Dad makes me so angry, too!" Instead: "I hear how angry you are with Dad, and I understand how hard it is for you. It's OK to feel angry."

Jealousy Is Normal

If your child has a close relationship with your ex and you feel jealous or resentful, it's easy to give into those demons and not your better angels.

Pausing to reflect on the real target of your anger and the underlying reason can help stop you from doing something that you'll regret later.

One parent often acts out anger toward their ex through the children. For example, your daughter loves a particular singer, and your ex secured two tickets to a sold-out concert. You know how much your daughter wants to go, but the concert falls during your custody weekend. Rather than allow your daughter to go to the concert with her father, you insist he give his ticket to you, or you won't permit your daughter to go. That kind of behavior hurts your ex, sure, but you're really hurting your child and your relationship with them.

Patience Is a Virtue

A divorce can be a long, drawn-out process, especially when custody and other issues around raising children are involved.

Managing the sadness, anger, irrational possessiveness, and the inevitable fallout of the process, as well as adjusting to a new normal—new homes, new rules, learning to coparent—require maturity and patience. You likely will hear statements that you don't like or agree with. You may be accused of actions that you may not have done. Requests and restrictions may send you into fight-or-flight mode. Dealing with all these elements requires you to dig deep and find empathy to fuel your patience with your ex and child.

The Blame Game

Blame is an especially complicated emotional reaction for parents and a way of protecting yourself from feeling vulnerable.[13] In most situations, both parents bear some responsibility for the breakup of a marriage. Even in cases of infidelity, unhappiness in the relationship is, with rare exceptions, the cause of the betrayal. This often means that there was conflict in the marriage that was not openly addressed. Blame transfers responsibility to someone else, while the blamer lacks or rejects an understanding of the whole picture. When you identify as a victim, you have no power or control in the situation. (This doesn't apply in cases of abuse or violence of course.)

Blame can be part of the mourning process. When we feel angry, hurt, rejected, or abandoned, we reflexively want someone or something to blame for the situation as a justification for those feelings. Confronted with loss, we need to make sense of that loss, and blame becomes a convenient bucket into which we pour those feelings. But to mix my metaphors, blame is more of a scheduled stop on the train ride of recovery from mourning—and not the last stop, either. In the end, you must take some responsibility for the dissolution of your marriage, or at least your part in it, to avoid similar painful situations in the future.

Blame also can be a way of sabotaging your child's relationship with their other parent. Whether conscious or unconscious, telling your kid that you blame your ex for the divorce or an unpleasant situation after it can drive a wedge between your ex and your child. This strategy puts your kid in the painful position of feeling obligated to choose a side, which easily can backfire.

CASE STUDY

Janet's mother came from a wealthy family and expected her husband to provide the same standard of living. As far as his wife was concerned, he never made enough money, *and* he neglected her because he worked long hours. After Janet's birth, her mother started drinking and lived in constant rage. Janet's father responded by having a series of affairs. His wife hired an expensive, vicious divorce lawyer. The mother received substantial spousal support, child support, and primary custody of their daughter. Janet stayed with her father two weekends per month and saw him after school on Wednesdays.

After the divorce, Janet's mother's drinking escalated; she went on endless tirades about the father. She divulged all the sordid details of her ex's affairs to Janet, now age 10. Janet's dad might not have been a good husband, but he was a good father, and Janet loved him. Even after the divorce, he made a point to attend all Janet's softball games, calling and texting her often. They shared a love of pizza and tried a different pizzeria every week.

Remarkably mature and clear-eyed, Janet knew that both her parents shared responsibility for the end of their marriage. She needed time away from them both to decide, going forward, what kind of relationship to have with each. Janet and her father reconciled. Unfortunately, her mother continued to blame and disparage her father, which Janet couldn't forgive, and finally Janet cut off contact with her mother.

When Your Child Reminds You of Your Ex

Your children are a blend of both of you and your ex. When you look at your children, you will see genetic features: your blue eyes or your ex's long legs. There are also less tangible but recognizable mannerisms: your ex's habit of twirling their hair when they're concentrating or your deep love of reading. These physical reminders of your former spouse can be challenging, particularly if you feel rejected, betrayed, or abandoned.

I am here to remind you that no matter how much of your ex you see in your child, they aren't your ex. Your child is a separate, unique individual. Recognizing this fact and keeping negative feelings about your ex separate from interactions with your child can define how well your child weathers the divorce. If you're struggling with this, see a therapist to help you work through it.

Competing for Your Child's Affection

Competing for your child's affection with presents and money, and/or being too permissive and relinquishing your authority as a parent in an attempt to "buy" their loyalty over the other parent is never a good idea. Children will begin to associate money and material things with the expression of love, rather than sharing time and experiences. Their need for presence and affection can turn into a bottomless pit of wanting things to replace love. They may carry this mindset into adulthood, where it will play out in their friendships and romantic relationships. It can turn into a game of one-upmanship with your ex—you bought Sean a bike? I'll buy him an ATV—and also stress you financially, especially if your circumstances have changed during or after the divorce. Letting your child dictate what you will or won't spend money on, or being too permissive, gives them power they should not have in your relationship with them.

Flexibility Goes Both Ways

Schedules and routines are critical for a child's emotional security, but being too rigid can cause problems, too. If an ex asks for or needs a reasonable change to the custody schedule, many parents respond with a knee-jerk: "No." But remember that flexibility goes both ways. You may need it in the future if you have a business trip or a last-minute dinner with friends. You may not be able to avoid conflict or disagreements all the time, but the more you can give (again, within reason), the more likely it is that you will receive. Awareness of your own insecurities and possessiveness and looking past your own needs to your child's will go a long way in terms of your child feeling loved by you and loving you in return.

For children, changes to the custody schedule often mean disappointment over lost time or experiences with a parent. Listen to their disappointment, but catch them with joy when you have them for longer or on holidays that you didn't expect. Make lemonade out of lemons for your children and make yourself the sweetest of lemonade.

Insecurity + Hurt Feelings = Defensiveness

We all defend ourselves against psychological and emotional pain. If your ex has hurt you, it makes sense to remain wary of or limit future interactions. It doesn't matter whether you initiated the divorce or your ex left. But proportion does matter because, in a divorce, defensiveness can become one of the most destructive behaviors.[14]

Defensiveness means hypervigilance and superreactivity to a perceived threat or insult. It anticipates a problem where none exists and strikes preemptively. It overreacts to reasonable requests. It continues the cycle of emotional aggression and violence that characterizes many divorces, often serving as a way to get back at your ex at the expense of your child. It short-circuits the possibility of a caring, or at least civil, relationship between former spouses.

Think of defensiveness as a form of PTSD. It can have many origins: fear of rejection, unresolved feelings, fear of being hurt or deceived again. If you have a history of loss or unhealthy relationships (family or romantic), you may default to defensiveness when dealing with your ex. Self-awareness (page 76) will help you avoid this kind of behavior. If that alone doesn't work, therapy can help.

But It's Not Fair

Focusing on winning an argument with an ex or insisting on tit for tat, rather than on what your child needs in the moment, loses sight of the real win: your child's emotional security, well-being, and happiness. Too often, exes obsess over what seems fair or equal time. Giving in on a point of contention—which parent has which holiday, who pays for what childcare or school expenses—can feel like losing, and losing feels bad. If arrangements fall apart, it's easy to feel resentful or impinged upon and project those feelings on to your child. Generosity begets generosity; possessiveness harms all relationships. In the long run, your child won't love you less if you spend one or two fewer days together. They *will* remember that you put aside your own need to win in favor of their need for security.

CASE STUDY

When Monica and Stewart divorced, they agreed on shared custody. Their three children, age 8, 11, and 15, stayed with Monica for three days a week and on alternate weekends. The parents worked out a complicated schedule for holidays and school vacations. Monica worked hard to create a new life as a single mom: taking on more responsibility at work, finding new friends, rekindling old friendships, and dating again. She enjoyed her time away from the children, not worrying about staying later at the office or childcare arrangements. She also took great pride in adhering to the custody agreement, making arrangements if conflicts arose in her schedule.

Stewart, on the other hand, had no problem asking Monica to take the kids if his time with them conflicted with work or social engagements. Monica considered her ex's requests selfish, and they imposed on her new-found freedom. When he called to change the custody schedule, she told him so in no uncertain terms. Unfortunately, she did this loudly and in front of the children, who interpreted these arguments as neither parent wanting them.

Monica's response to Stewart's schedule changes was understandable, but it also damaged her relationship with her children. She was able to separate her resentments about accommodating Stewart's schedule without his doing the same for her, from her feelings for her children. She recognized that her additional time with them was a gift, not a burden. To help repair her relationship with them, she explained that she always wanted to be with them, and her reaction to their father's requests had more to do with adjusting to their absence and protecting herself from her own sadness when they had to leave. The kids accepted her explanation and were better able to tell her when they felt hurt or rejected by her reactions.

Be Generous with Money

Parents often obsess over the fairness of the divorce agreement, especially when it comes to money. All too often, they use it as a weapon or means of control. It should go without saying, but experience has proven that it needs saying: Keep financial squabbles between adults.

Prioritizing your child above the pettiness of financial arrangements offers another way of being your best self. When a parent refuses to contribute to their child's care because it's "not fair" for them to pay for them, or when parents involve their children by telling them, "I am not paying for X; that is your mom's responsibility," they are hurting their children and damaging their relationship with them.

CASE STUDY

When Karen and Drew divorced, the agreement gave them fifty-fifty custody of their two daughters, Pamela, 12, and Kiera, 14, as well as shared decision-making for health issues and education. Kiera had learning issues and was being bullied at school. Karen wanted to send her to a small private school for better educational support and a fresh social start. Drew wanted Kiera to tough it out, even though Kiera's therapist strongly recommended the change.

Karen and Drew worked with me, but we hit a dead end in terms of reaching an agreement on how to pay for Kiera's school. Although a stretch, Karen could afford the school on her own. I recommended that she not let her anger toward Drew or an attachment to "fairness" prevent her from doing what was right for Kiera. Fortunately, Karen recognized that waiting for Drew to agree to share tuition costs only postponed what was best for their daughter. Karen agreed to pay the full tuition if Drew agreed to let Kiera attend the school, which he did.

Kiera quickly settled into her new school. The warm, supportive staff welcomed her, and she found a group of friends who shared her interest in theater. Karen never regretted the decision. She remained angry at her ex, but she didn't let that anger prevent her from doing what was best for her children.

Don't Overshare with Your Children

Children, even adolescents, aren't mini adults. They're not your friend, confidante, or therapist. You're the parent, and that means acting like an adult. Your child leans on you for stability, not the other way around. Don't overshare your feelings, fears, or insecurities about the divorce or being alone.[15] Put drinking, using drugs, talking about your sex life, conflicts with your ex or any romantic partner, and discussing your loneliness well out of bounds. Don't be like the mother who discusses her ex's gambling and porn addiction with her 19-year-old daughter and asks her for dating advice.

No one expects you to put on a happy face all the time. Showing your children that you are occasionally sad, angry, or frustrated is human. It also models for your child how an adult handles those emotions. But frequency and intensity matter. Adult emotions and reactions belong in adult spaces, which is why everyone going through a divorce should go to therapy.

Your Child Is Not Your Spy

You may be curious about your children's time with your ex. Asking, "How was dinner with Dad?" is fine. Asking, "What did you do this weekend at Mom's?" is also fine. Pumping your kid for information about your ex's new significant other, how much your ex spent on birthday gifts for their new stepchild, or whether Dad is fighting with his new wife, is not OK.

When your child returns from your ex's home, your questions should stay focused on your child's experiences and feelings and should not be an attempt to ferret out information that you can use against your ex or that will make you feel jealous or envious. Let your kid know that they can talk to you about any feelings or worries and that you're there to help them work things out. Don't compel your child to share anything that will make them feel uncomfortable or guilty, unless you have real reason to suspect there is neglect or abuse.

CASE STUDY

Noah's parents divorced when he was 8 years old. His mother demanded that he report back on everything that happened when he was with his father and, later, his father's girlfriend. Noah did as she instructed, but he felt disloyal to his father. He also liked the woman who eventually became his stepmother.

At age 28, Noah began therapy with me. He was struggling with his mother's continuing, voracious need to know everything about his father's life and why he left her for "that floozy." Noah worked on setting limits with his mother, and it took some time before she understood that he no longer would spy

> for her. Noah confessed to his father that he had felt guilty for many years and apologized. His father and stepmother understood the difficulty of the position that Noah's mother had put him in. They told him that they loved him and encouraged him to forgive himself.

It's Not About You

Sometimes, your child will prefer you and sometimes they will prefer your ex. Sometimes, your kid will want to share their feelings with you and sometimes they will want to keep things to themselves. Sometimes, they'll want to leave early to go to your ex or stay later. The ebb and flow of parent-child relationships that feel normal (if frustrating), when married, can become fraught with meaning after a divorce.

Your feelings of rejection and disappointment are normal. Everyone who goes through a divorce has weak or vulnerable moments. Making your child feel guilty because you feel lonely or counting on them to keep you company isn't healthy. Again, you're the parent. Taking life in stride and not overreacting to your child's moods or preferences provides security and reassurance; often they are testing you to see whether your love really is unconditional. If you feel insecure about being loved by your child, use your support system to vent and get reassurance from other adults.

Don't Isolate Your Child from Extended Family

Losing your nuclear family is one thing, but losing your extended family is a double blow. When children lose a parent because of divorce, other adult family members often step in to help them feel loved. Children close to or cared for by grandparents, aunts, and uncles feel greater loss when a parent limits or forbids them to spend time with those family members.

You might confuse your anger at your ex with anger at their parents and/or siblings. Unless you have a very good reason to do so, be generous and encourage your child's connection to that extended family. They can help to support you and are more people in this world who can offer your children unconditional love and loving connection.

CASE STUDY

Kaye had a difficult childhood. Her father became a drug addict, and when she was 7 years old, her mother divorced him. She didn't see her dad again for 20 years, until she sat by his bed while he was dying. In the meantime, Kaye's mother worked two jobs to support her and her brother. Always exhausted, her mother had a short temper and didn't give her children much affection. Before the divorce, Kaye had a close relationship with her father's mother, who gave her the warmth and affection she was missing at home. The worst part of the divorce, Kaye told me, was that her mother refused to let her see her paternal grandmother and that she couldn't stop blaming her mother for that loss.

Signs You May Not Be Doing OK

It should not be a surprise that you may not be your best self through the divorce process. When people suffer a loss or trauma, such as divorce, they often become anxious or depressed.[16] If you are increasingly irritable or impatient, have trouble sleeping or sleep too much and have difficulty getting out of bed, can't control your temper, lose your appetite, have panic attacks, or struggle to function through the day, speak with a mental health professional. If you're caring for your children's physical needs but can't engage with them emotionally, either through conversation or play, you may be suffering from depression and you need treatment. Don't beat yourself up over these symptoms. See them as a sign that you need help. Stoically going it alone won't help you or your child.

Reaching Out for Help

I consider therapy an essential component of the support system of anyone going through a divorce. I encourage clients to also enlist a close friend (or friends) as a "divorce buddy," a trustworthy shoulder to cry on, to validate or challenge your feelings and actions, to give you an unvarnished assessment of what you're doing right or could improve with your kid.

But even the closest, most loving friends can't replace a therapist. Why? Because everyone has their own feelings and biases about you, your ex, and that relationship. Therapists train to keep their personal feelings separate from their work. They have your back and are on your side, but they can remain truly objective and not project their own emotional baggage on you in a way that close friends often can't.

I like to think of therapy as a way of sitting shivah, a Jewish mourning ritual. For one week, mourners sit, reflect, tell stories about their loved one, and mourn. A therapist can help you mourn not only the loss of your spouse and your marriage, but also the past losses intertwined with your current loss. In that safe space, you can explore all the feelings that you're afraid to express to others.

Sometimes, a divorce isn't simply an end, but rather a new beginning of a better life and a better version of ourselves. But we can't do it alone; we need many hands. Divorce is painful; it can also be empowering. Even when a change isn't what we anticipated or wanted, it can be an opportunity for personal growth and a step toward becoming our best selves.

7

REPAIRING TRUST AND HEALING TRAUMA

Even if you do everything right and your divorce goes smoothly, remember that it has shaken your child's world deeply. Losing their nuclear family and adjusting to new transitions between households will cause uncertainty and anxiety about the future.

It's your job to help your child regain steady emotional footing and learn to trust you. It's your ex's job, too, but we'll focus on you for this chapter. Repair requires establishing stability, continuity, routine, and consistency as quickly as possible. Let's review what you can do to foster the healing process and mend the tear in the fabric of your child's sense of security.

Being There

Guiding children through divorce requires physical and emotional presence. That means prioritizing them—not work and not your social life. It means engaging with them when they want or need you, not just when it's convenient. Your ex may not make the same kind of commitment to good parenting as you do. In that case, focus on what you can do, not what your ex can't or won't do. The Serenity Prayer can come in handy here: Change what you can, accept what you can't, and find peace.

For most of us, work occupies the biggest amount of time outside family. During divorce proceedings and until your child has adjusted to a custody schedule and new routines, rethink your work arrangements to focus on your family. Let your employer know what's happening and that you'll need flexibility and/or time off. Ask whether you can work from home on days when you have custody. If possible, curtail travel for work. These days, video conferencing can replace almost all business travel, at least for a while. If you do need to travel, schedule regular video calls with your kid. Even babies recognize their parents' voices and faces. Don't schedule any other appointments or engagements on custody days. Many divorcing parents project onto their children more resilience than they actually have. Don't do that, either. If you need to leave your kid in someone's care, look to family or a familiar caregiver. If financially feasible, consider working part-time or taking a sabbatical.

As much as possible, drop them off and pick them up—from school, therapy appointments, after-school activities, doctors' appointments, socializing with friends, everything. Be there for transitions: waking, leaving the house, coming home from school, custody pickups and drop-offs, and going to sleep.

Consider scaling back your schedule and your child's until the new routines feel secure. Don't be shy about canceling plans if necessary. Time for yourself also matters, so when you don't have custody, schedule nights out with friends and weekends away. These temporary changes represent a sacrifice for everyone on multiple levels, but they'll pay off in terms of your child's wellness and your happiness and satisfaction as a parent.

Baby Them a Little

Even secure, mature children may seek comfort during a divorce by regressing a little. Doing that gives them the psychological space to rebuild their emotional resilience.[1] A potty-trained toddler may want to wear a diaper or bottle feed. A school-age child may ask to be cared for like a toddler. Bed wetting and tantrums may return, or a school phobia may develop. A teenager might "get sick" more often to stay home. Kids of all ages may want to crawl into bed, watch movies, and eat ice cream.

All of them, even young adults, need physical affection to heal. It provides a feeling of bodily security and safety, lowers cortisol and stress levels, and lowers their pulse and breathing rate.[2] Adolescents may reject hugs or physical touch, but let them know that you're available when *they* want to cuddle.

Getting children to sleep may become more challenging.[3] Sleep is a separation and even older children can have separation issues. Prepare for sleepless nights. After a divorce, many parents let their children sleep with them for a full year to rebuild a sense of security. If your child is having sleep issues, you could sleep in their room on an extra bed or mattress on the floor. There's no perfect time to transition kids back to their own room. Sometimes they'll readjust on their own because sleeping in the same room with you eventually becomes uncomfortable or they miss their own bed. Other times, you'll need to initiate the change. It may be two steps forward and one back until they sleep alone or in their own beds. Don't rush this process.

Focus on Feelings

Children need their parents to hear and validate their feelings.[4] Doing that successfully means reading cues that indicate sadness, anger, or frustration. Don't let the moment pass. Verbalizing that you notice their feelings can open the door for an important conversation. It also represents the greatest recognition and acknowledgement of your child's value as a person.

When no one acknowledges children's emotions, they don't feel seen or important. Putting their feelings into words matters because asking them why they're feeling what they're feeling is often useless. Most children, adolescents, and—let's face it—even adults don't know why they're feeling what they're feeling. Some may have trouble identifying *what* they're feeling, especially if stressed (both good reasons for therapy). Use your imagination to put their feelings and the possible motivation for their feelings into words. For instance, "I wonder if you're upset because Dad canceled this weekend and won't be at your concert/game?"

The phrase "I wonder" helps because it doesn't make assumptions. Saying, "I know you're sad/angry," automatically excludes other feelings. Reflective statements—"You seem sad. I wonder if it's because..." "You sound angry. I wonder if it's because..." "You look frustrated. I wonder if it's because..."—gives kids the option to walk through the door or not. Giving them that choice matters.

Keeping a stiff upper lip may work for some adults, but it's harmful to children. Encouraging and eliciting feelings from children helps them heal. Encourage them to express their feelings, good and bad. That may mean having to hear, acknowledge, and process accusations, rage, despair, and hopelessness, much of it directed at you. Think of yourself as an emotional recycling plant in which your kid can deposit painful feelings for recycling into safety, love, and hope. Reflect their emotions and reassure them that all their feelings, even the negative ones, are acceptable and you'll love them no matter what. Their greatest comfort will come from knowing that you can handle all their emotions, whatever they're feeling, so reassure them often.[5]

Taking Responsibility

For children going through a divorce, anger matters just as much for the mourning process as it does for adults. Kids may need someone to blame for the unwanted changes to their lives. Your child may give you cues or tell you, flat out, that it's your fault. Denying responsibility will salt the wound. If you can't absorb your child's anger and accept responsibility that you and your ex caused what's happening, they'll turn that blame on themselves.

The most important first step in any healing process is that the person who hurt the injured party takes responsibility, regardless of whether the hurt was intentional. A parent saying, "I understand the divorce has changed your life, and I'm sorry," will begin the healing process. Something like, "I'm sorry, but..." focuses on excuses, dismisses the other person's pain, and negates the apology. This isn't the time to justify your decisions or assign blame. It doesn't matter why you divorced or who initiated the break. It doesn't matter whether your child understands that, in the long run, splitting was the best move. The divorce itself, not the reason(s) for it, hurt your child.

Don't Wait to Get Your Children Help

Seeking help from a mental health professional can feel like an admission that you caused the pain that your children are feeling. Taking a wait-and-see approach doesn't work. It only delays the healing process. The sooner you treat a wound, physical or emotional, the easier it is to prevent infection and the more quickly it will heal. Children need their parents to be there for them, but if the parents caused the pain, kids may find it hard to express, communicate, or process it without outside help.

Therapists aren't one-size-fits-all. When interviewing them, ask about training *after* their degree. Therapists specializing in children and adolescents come from different backgrounds. They can be social workers, psychologists, or psychiatrists. They also can be licensed marital and family therapists. These categories mean nothing in terms of their expertise. They signify only that the person is licensed by the state and can receive reimbursement from insurance. What matters is their postgraduate experience and whether they were in treatment themselves as a requirement of their postgraduate training. It's *very* important to find a therapist who has gone through extensive therapy themselves, as part of their training, so they've worked through their own losses or conflicts so they can treat your child or family without biases or preconceptions.

Therapists act like safe-deposit boxes for children's feelings when they can't express them to their parents. Each child should have their own therapist so they have their own individual safe place. Lumping all your kids into the same therapy or with the same therapist is like putting them all into the same activity, regardless of age, interests, or skills. Take the time to find a good match for each of your kids. Certain circumstances, such as sibling rivalry issues, parental favoritism, or other interpersonal conflicts between or among family members, require family therapy, meaning that family members are all seen together or in specific groups, but that shouldn't replace individual sessions.

Different kinds of treatment work better, depending on the child's age. Start with a play or talk therapist who is psychoanalytically or psychodynamically oriented. Psychodynamic therapy seeks to understand how relationships and personal history affect personality.[6] Children under age eight will benefit most from some kind of play therapy in which they can express feelings through play and artwork, because that's the language of children.[7] After that age and until they're 13 or 14, kids become better able to talk about their feelings, but they may prefer to engage using board games or physical games such as mini-hoop basketball. This kind of side-by-side play often leads to trusting conversation about their feelings.

In talk therapy, older teens may talk a *lot*, very little, or alternate between the two extremes. Even if they talk a lot, that doesn't mean that they're revealing their true feelings. They might be using verbal diarrhea to avoid acknowledging or thinking about their feelings. It can take months for older teens to trust a therapist and open up.

Cognitive behavioral therapy helps when kids struggle to express their feelings openly. The behavioral techniques can help with some anxiety, but depression requires uncovering deeper feelings and motivations.[8] Dialectic behavioral therapy is used for the most nonverbal of teens, age 14 and up, who need structure and even workbooks to uncover feelings that they can't articulate.[9]

At age 14 or 15, kids often don't want their parents to speak to their therapist, or vice versa. Most therapists respect those wishes, with a few important exceptions. The teens who I treat know that our sessions are confidential and that I'll speak to their parents only with their permission *unless* serious threats to their safety become apparent: suicidal thoughts, violent fantasies and/or plans to enact them, taking extreme risks, or substance abuse. Most of the adolescents I work with allow me to continue working with their parents as long as I'm up front about it. Some even bring a parent to work through specific conflicts.

Some older children and teens will refuse to see a therapist. If they're not visibly anxious or depressed, not isolating from friends, and not struggling with schoolwork, you can take a watch-and-wait approach. If those symptoms materialize, make an appointment with an appropriate therapist. When kids feel vulnerable, they may prove more willing to accept help. If you have real reason to think that they may hurt themselves or others, that's a medical emergency. Take them to the emergency room immediately for a psychological evaluation.

Guidance counselors, school social workers, and pastoral counselors also can play a role in healing your family and your child. It's often easier for kids, particularly older ones, to go to a guidance counselor or school social worker during the school day. That person can help as a bridge to therapy and offer support for kids reluctant to go to an appointment outside school hours. Some schools organize groups for kids from divorced families in which they can connect with others going through the same experience. If a group like this is available, encourage but don't push your child to join it. Groups like this may be available at neighboring schools, mental health clinics, or community centers. If not, suggest to your school, community center, or place of worship that they create one.

Again, parent guidance forms an integral part of child therapy. You hold the keys to helping your child weather the divorce. A therapist can help you understand what your kid needs and improve your communication and parenting skills.

Turn Down the Volume

To take unnecessary pressure off your child, you need to regulate everything else that creates stress. Reevaluate what truly matters and turn down the volume on expectations for academics, socializing, and extracurricular activities. If your 12-year-old was a high achiever in school but their grades have dropped, *don't* insist on more time studying. Let your child know that lower marks are OK for the time being. Maybe your child was a star basketball player or first violin in the school orchestra, but now they don't want to go to practice.

Sometimes, they'll tell you directly, and sometimes you need to read their behavior. Fatigue, bad moods, and changes to sleep or eating patterns offer the clearest signals. Let them know that it's OK to take a break. Just as you've been reevaluating what's important to you as you make a new life, your child is doing the same. It doesn't mean they won't go back. If they do abandon a sport or activity that they were passionate about, remember that kids' interests change frequently.

The More, the Merrier

You can't have too many people in your life who love you. Spending time with loving family, extended family, and good friends will help heal you and reassure your kids.

Take the opportunity of your divorce to reevaluate your support system. Family means many things, and love doesn't have an exclusive agreement with blood relatives. Chosen family may prove more reliable, caring, and loving than your family of origin. Just because your parents, grandparents, or siblings live nearby doesn't mean that they'll make you feel loved or good about yourself. If they're critical, judgmental, angry, or depressed, stay away. But if they're loving and kind, the more, the merrier.

Kids going through a divorce commonly worry that they'll be alone if something happens to one or both parents. Strengthening relationships with aunts, uncles, or cousins can help kids with these worries, particularly only children. On vacation or school holidays, consider staying with relatives or extended family to help your child adjust to the shift and reassure them that they always will have people around them who will love and care for them.

Rebuilding Trust

Divorce breaks an unspoken promise to children of raising them in a secure, stable, loving family. When you divorce, you need to rebuild trust and repair that broken promise.

Rebuilding your child's trust in you means exercising extreme sensitivity about other changes during the divorce process and in the first year after. Again, change as little as possible, as slowly as possible. If you have control over your living arrangements, don't move, change their school, or get rid of a pet. Maintaining stability provides a sense of continuity and consistency and will help your child understand that you're keeping other promises, spoken and unspoken, too.

The biggest break in trust comes from cutting the invisible thread that binds a family. Bringing a new partner into the picture too soon rubs salt in the wound. You may feel excited to share your new happiness, but let your child grieve for a long while before adding another person to the mix.

Make only the promises you can keep, and keep the ones you make. If you're not sure, saying, "Of course we can go to Disney World for Christmas," "Yes, we'll spend Thanksgiving together," or "We'll never sell the house" sets them up for disappointment that will shake their trust in you. Honesty puts pennies in the piggy bank of trust: "I can't promise, but I'll do my best" or "I don't know, but I'll tell you as soon as I do." They may not like the answer, but you get points for honesty.

Unfortunately, you may have to break a promise on occasion. When that happens, don't delay telling your child. Waiting only makes it worse. Be prepared for your child to be unhappy, disappointed, or even furious at you. Remember, it's your job to listen and empathize with their feelings. Say that you're sorry and don't make excuses. No "buts" about it! Calmly explain what happened and take responsibility. This is the beginning of repair.

New Rituals and Celebrations

Divorce can mean losing family rituals and traditions. Maybe you always opened one present each on Christmas Eve, Mom made pancakes every Sunday, or the kids always visited your ex's mother in the summer. These traditions may change because of the realities of living between two homes. New arrangements create room for new traditions, while keeping (many of) the old ones. If being a short-order cook isn't your idea of a fun Sunday, substitute a run for donuts, muffins, or bagels. If the other parent gets Christmas Day, have a special dinner and open one present on Christmas Eve at your home. On the day that your kid returns to your care, have dinner at a particular restaurant, extend bedtime by an extra story, or watch a favorite movie or TV show together.

Celebrations are always important, and especially so after a divorce. Celebrate birthdays; graduations—even from nursery school and kindergarten; and all the holidays, secular and religious. Look for other reasons, too: you or your children's successes or accomplishments, even the smallest ones; the first and last day of school; first lost tooth; return from sleepaway camp, Wednesday night, you name it. There's no occasion so small that you can't make the most of it with ice cream after dinner (or as dinner).

Get a Pet

Researchers have extensively documented the healing power of pets. Having a pet can lower blood pressure, increase production of oxytocin (the "love" hormone), decrease production of cortisol (a stress hormone), and improve mental health and mindfulness.[10] Caring for a pet teaches kids compassion, empathy, patience, responsibility, selflessness, and other invaluable life skills.

If the family pet stayed with your ex, get one for your home. It's not just for the kids. If you don't already have a family pet, consider getting one. Cats and dogs are obvious choices for cuddly companions, but other animals—fish, turtles, birds, and small mammals, such as a hamster, guinea pig, or rabbit—can be loved buddies, too. Children may be messy, rebellious, and uncooperative at times, but we parents get used to the chaos of their company and miss them when they're not there. When your kid is with your ex, a pet may create additional responsibility, but it also can offer emotional support for you.

It Gets Better

Healing isn't linear. It has no predictable timeline. Children all heal in their own way, in their own time.

After the beginning of a divorce, it takes at least a year for children to find their balance. Look for signs that children are returning to a semblance of normality. They may seem less anxious, distractible, moody, or touchy. If they shunned physical contact, they may brush up against you or lean in while walking the dog or watching TV. The embargo on talking about their day, drama with friends, or struggles at school might come to a sudden end. They may take pleasure again in activities or interests from before the split, becoming more engaged in school or with friends and family. This stage can feel like a dark cloud lifting and the sun finally reemerging.

Keep in mind, however, that children's and teens' emotional weather is as inconsistent and unpredictable as atmospheric weather. The sun won't keep shining all the time. Dark clouds will return at some point. But if you can keep the conflict with your ex to a minimum and give your child space to enjoy life as a child, you all will enjoy more sunny days than stormy ones.

8

NEW PARTNERS AND BLENDED FAMILIES

When you have children, dating has its challenges. Finding a new partner means getting back into the pool, a task no easier in your 40s or 50s than in your 20s. But now, you have to manage not just your own hopes and expectations but also the logistics of custody, childcare, and your child's feelings. You want a loving supportive partner for yourself as well as a loving stepparent for your kid. The situation gets even more complicated if your new partner has children, too.

The Fantasy of Reunion

Almost all children over age three harbor the fantasy that their parents will get back together. Just as you may be wistful at times about the marriage that didn't fulfill your own hopes and the family you have lost, they, too, may be sad over the breakup and the missed potential for an ideal family, even if they never had it.

As long as you remain single, the fantasy of that reunion remains alive, regardless of whether your child acknowledges it. Spending time separately with a new partner or bringing one home breaks through the defenses of denial, and your child likely will mourn the loss of the fantasy, taking out those feelings of anger and hurt on you. When your four-year-old says, "I miss Daddy," or your teen erupts in anger because you forgot to pack their cleats and yells, "This wouldn't have happened if Mom was here!" they're not saying that they love you less but that they miss the way life used to be. Replying, "I miss our family, too," or acknowledging that, yes, their mother probably wouldn't have forgotten to pack a missing item and you'll make a note to remember next time, shows that you're listening. It also models that it's OK to be vulnerable and admit your mistakes and limitations.

Introducing a New Partner

Having your child meet a stream of new love interests is a mistake on many levels. Children crave consistency and reliability. Divorce shows them that relationships can break beyond repair and that loved and trusted people can leave. In the aftermath of a divorce, they feel unsafe and will be suspicious of any prospective new partner for you who might become an additional parent for them.

Yes, it can be frustrating and even burdensome to lead two lives, one with your kid and, one with your romantic partner, but you need to do exactly that until you and your new partner commit to each other exclusively. Repercussions always follow introducing a new person into your child's life. It's only worth doing if you feel the two of you have a future.

Timing can help your child absorb the news. This isn't an "Oh, by the way" conversation. As with other major news, don't do it on the fly; give them some time to react and ask questions. Remember, you're about to disrupt their life again, even if it's for the better in the long run. Consider what's going on in their lives before you have this discussion. Avoid times of school or social stress or long separations from you, such as sleepaway camp or vacations with your ex.

Don't be surprised if your child already has an idea that you're involved with someone new. Older kids are especially quick to pick up on clues: trouble reaching you while they're with your ex, sensing that you seem happier or your mood seems lighter, your not taking certain calls when you're with them. Tell your ex about your new companion *before* introducing them to your kid. Your ex should hear it from you, rather than your child.

After you deliver the news, let the idea marinate before you introduce them to your new significant other. Keep the first few meetings casual, brief, and low key. Invite your new companion to join you on a weekend family activity, such as a movie, an outing in the park, or a weeknight dinner at your kid's favorite restaurant. A neutral location is best, and including your new love interest in an activity makes side-by-side conversation easier. Give your child time to acclimate and hopefully accept your new person. If it goes well on both sides, you can increase the number and duration of the visits and add occasions with other family members and friends present, like your child concert, game, or recital.

Under the best circumstances, infants and toddlers may act fearful, clingy, or fussy when meeting new people. Be patient and ask your new partner to be patient as well. Schedule first visits to occur when your child is awake and alert—so, not right before or after nap time or later in the evening when they are tired or cranky.

Hold your baby or let your toddler sit on your lap. Don't hand off your little one immediately. Your new partner can make eye contact and talk to your child softly but shouldn't touch them at first. Let your child lead and watch for cues that your baby is open to playing peekaboo or that your toddler will welcome a companion for playing with blocks.

When you have custody, avoid overnights until confirming that the new relationship has become a long-term commitment. That doesn't necessarily mean marriage, just that both adults are in it for the long haul. Adult sleepovers involve locked doors, unusual sounds from the bedroom, and awkward periods of adjustment for everyone. Let your child know in advance: "Paul is going to sleep over one or two nights a week. How do you feel about that?" They may react with a shrug and no comment or express happiness that you're in a serious relationship. They also may object. If that's the reaction, ask them for more information about what they're feeling and listen carefully.

- "I can see that you're not happy about Sharon sleeping over, and I want to understand why. Can you tell me what you're feeling about it?"
- "I hear that you may not be ready to have Carl stay over. I wonder, is there anything that I or they can do to make you feel more comfortable?"
- "I understand that you feel sad and angry that Sophia is staying over. Maybe it feels like I'm moving on from your mom, but you know you always come first."

Ask whether you can do anything to make the transition easier.

- "Would it help if David stayed over only once or twice per week for now?"
- "Would it help if Lia came over after dinner or left before you woke up?"

If your child reacts to your new companion sleeping over: shows signs of stress, such as depression, panic attacks, withdrawing from you or friends, or increased aggression toward you, your new partner, siblings, or friends, seriously consider postponing overnight visits until they can adjust to your new love. In the end, however, *you're* the parent, and you're integrating this new person into your family. You have a right to a romantic life, so remember that these accommodations are transitional. Eventually, your child needs to adjust. It's about timing.

Infants and toddlers won't understand what a grownup sleepover entails, but don't be surprised to hear "Are you guys having *sex?*" or "Eww, *gross!*" from school-age or adolescent kids. Even kids who like your new partner may express anger or resentment that they have to share you with someone new. The more of an effort your new partner makes to show interest in your child and not judge their emotional reactions, the more quickly your child will accept your new partner.

Don't introduce your new partner to your child by including them on a vacation or by announcing, "This is my new girl (or boy) friend, who is moving in with us next week." That's exactly what has happened with many parents whom I've treated. In more than one case, parents feel so guilty about having a new love that they waited until just before remarrying to tell their children. Don't be that parent.

Relief Over Your Happiness

Children can see the physical and emotional impact of divorce. I always tell parents even if you were an Academy Award–winning actor, you couldn't hide your true feelings from your children: They read your facial expression and your body language, they hear the tone of your voice and listen to your words. They're know when you are hurt, lonely, or depressed. Regardless of whether they tell you, they worry about you.

As any adult with aging parents knows, concern about the well-being of parents can become a heavy emotional burden. Many grownups have the cognitive and emotional tools to handle it, but kids don't. When children worry about you, it makes it harder for them to separate. They may take on the role of friend and companion rather than spreading their wings and creating their own social life. Adolescents and young adults may postpone pursuing a romantic life of their own, especially only children. If you are happily dating or part of a new couple, it can relieve the burden of worry that they might be carrying, plus any guilt for wanting that burden lifted.

Symmetry matters to kids. When one parent moves on with their romantic life, children often want the other parent to do so as well. When one parent is lonely and the other seems fine, kids often feel responsible for making the lonely parent happy. It's a delicate balance to both reassure your children that they are the most important thing in your life, but that when they are away you are OK.

CASE STUDY

Casey's dad told him that he had a new girlfriend. Maya, Casey's mother, wasn't dating anyone, but she had no issue with her ex seeing someone new. Casey, age 12, liked his dad's girlfriend and had a good time when he stayed with them, but felt guilty about leaving his mother alone. He called her often to check on her and occasionally cut short visits with his father. After several months of this behavior, Maya sat Casey down to talk. She explained that, yes, she missed him when he was gone. But she also enjoyed having the time to see friends, to go to cultural events, and to start dating herself. Knowing that his mother was busy with activities that made her happy left Casey free to enjoy his time with his dad without feeling guilty.

Jealousy Is Natural

Although your children may be relieved and happy to see you happy, it's not uncommon for them to be jealous of a new romantic partner. Even in an intact marriage, many children unconsciously want to have you for themselves. We mental health professionals call this an oedipal victory. Sigmund Freud famously described the relationship that all children between the ages of three and six have with their opposite-sex parent; our first experience of romantic love is with that parent. When a three-year-old boy says, "Mommy, I want to marry you and send Daddy away," or a four-year-old girl says, "Daddy, I want to run away with you, and let's leave Mommy in the closet," we recognize this response as normal and temporary. Shortly after age five, children realize that marrying their parent isn't possible. They accept that reality and decide to learn the ways of the other parent to attract a partner of their own. When parents divorce, there's no longer competition for Mom or Dad's affection and attention. Younger children may revert to wanting to sleep in your bed, and you may have a hard time getting them back to their own room. They also may become intensely jealous if you start another romantic relationship.

With young children, the best way to handle this development is to encourage them to tell you how they feel. Explain that you can love different people in different ways and that, no matter how many people you love, your heart always has room for more love. The love that you have for them is special, though, and what you feel for your new partner is different. Tell them how much you love them and that you always will love them.

Go out of your way to show your child, no matter how old, that you're not abandoning them for your new companion. School-age and adolescent kids are far from the oedipal triangle of toddlerhood, but you may see remnants of some of that conflict in them.[1] This is especially true if you had long-standing problems with your ex. Even young adults who have moved on and have a romantic life of their own may express jealousy and ambivalence toward your new love.

CASE STUDY

Sybil and Andrew divorced amicably and worked hard to coparent Susan, their 8-year-old daughter, with as little disagreement between them and stress on her as possible. They agreed to wait a full year before dating or bringing a significant other into Susan's life.

Shortly after that year ended, Andrew met and quickly fell in love with Carina. Andrew told Sybil that he had met someone for whom he cared greatly, and he saw a future with her. He wanted to introduce her to Susan. Sybil appreciated that Andrew told her first. Six months later, Carina had become a regular fixture in Andrew's life, so Susan's parents agreed that it was time for Susan to meet her. All the adults were on the same page.

Susan had other ideas, however. Since her parent's divorce, so much had changed in her life, and she didn't want more change. She would have preferred that her parents had stayed together, but having them, separately, to herself also worked for her. When Andrew told Susan about Carina, Susan felt betrayed by her father and angry at her mother, who seemed perfectly fine with her father's new girlfriend. At first, Susan refused to meet Carina. When both parents insisted that they meet, she was cold and curt, giving one-word answers when Carina asked her about school and her hobbies. When Carina suggested that they play Monopoly, Susan literally turned her back.

Andrew and Sybil came to me to discuss the situation, and I recommended that Susan see a therapist. There, Susan expressed her fears of losing her dad and that her mother would not be long in finding a new relationship of her own. Andrew and Sybil reassured Susan that she always would remain their priority and that her time with each parent would remain sacred.

Andrew shared all this information with Carina, who understood Susan's fears and jealousy. Secure in Andrew's affection, Carina gave Andrew and Susan the time and space that they needed. Susan's story had a happy ending because, through her parents' and Carina's patience and sensitivity, she eventually saw the benefits of having a smart, athletic stepmother who loved Mexican food as much as she did.

When you're in a new relationship, make sure to spend time alone with your child rather than always including your partner. Ask your child whether they need more time with you or want you to check in more often. When children receive enough of their parents' time and attention, they feel less jealous of others. It's the same at age 2 or 22.

At the same time, it's also important for children to accept that adults need separate adult time. Emphasize the importance of parents being happy in their adult lives so children can flourish, develop, and ultimately have lives of their own.

Expect Anger

Kids thrive on routine and predictability.[2] Divorce brings unwelcome changes, so predictable routines become especially important for their emotional stability. A new person in the mix changes the family structure and routine, so kids don't always experience it as rainbows and unicorns. Even if they're happy for you, resentment toward your new partner and anger at you for bringing a new person into their lives can color their emotional landscape. Younger children can become physically aggressive: hitting, biting, or kicking. Older children and adolescents may go radio silent or become verbally and emotionally abusive.

My grandmother, a wise woman, used to say, "Better out than in," and she was right. It's better for children to express their anger openly than to turn away or internalize those feelings.[3] If kids feel safe enough to express those feelings, that's good—within certain limits of course. Child therapists often tell first-time patients, "Words are helpful. You can say anything you want, but you can't physically hurt me, hurt yourself, or break the furniture." That's a good guideline for parents, too. As long as your child is using words and not acting out aggression, let them say what they need to say, how they need to say it. You can handle it.

If you introduce your five-year-old son to your new boyfriend and your child lashes out by hitting and biting, resist the urge to punish him. Take him aside and tell him that you can see how hard it is for him to meet this new person and that meeting any new person can be hard. Sometimes, it can make us angry or afraid. Acknowledging his feelings can help him regulate his emotions. If, after learning that you have a new girlfriend, your teenage daughter tells you that she doesn't want to visit this weekend or says that your new girlfriend is awful and she hates her, don't panic. Be patient. Tell her that you understand that it may take time. Also consider this line that I always recommend to parents: "You don't have to love or even like my new person. You don't have to like that I have a new person. But you do have to respect that I love her, and treat her with respect and civility." In the end, you can't control how your child feels about your new partner, but you can request respect for you and your choice to be with them.

What If Your Child Doesn't Accept Your New Partner?

Eventually, most children come to accept, like, and often love a parent's new partner or their stepparents. In some cases, however, children never accept the "interloper," who they see as competition or a replacement for the other parent. For these children, a divorce is just too traumatic, and the only control they have over a situation that is out of their control is to hold onto their anger and raise their emotional barriers to closeness. They may refuse to play nice with a new love interest. Even if they secretly have fond feelings for a new partner, they may never allow themselves to express them openly.

A stepparent's behavior has a lot to do with how your child will embrace them—literally and figuratively. Is your new partner competitive, critical, dismissive, judgmental, rejecting, or strict? Overly solicitous or intrusive? Do they love bomb your child with toys, tech, or attention in order to be accepted or loved immediately? These actions may trigger mistrust or rejection from your kid. If that happens, the burden falls on your partner and you to speak to a professional for couples therapy to work out any unexpected feelings of resentment and jealousy.

If you're the stepparent, your own insecurities can make a kid's rejection sting even more. Expecting a little emotional discomfort can make rejection a bit easier to take. If you can take it in stride, you may eventually earn your stepchild's respect and even affection. Overreacting will have lasting effects on your relationship.

Blending a family is a lot like trying to make salad dressing. You can't blend oil and water without them separating, but you can do it if you know what ingredients to add, in what measure, and how to mix them.

CASE STUDY

Sam, a warm, easy-going, affectionate father, prioritized his daughters, Karen, 17, and Marisa, 19, who still lived at home. He wanted to spend as much time with them as possible before they left the nest. Sam's new girlfriend, Anna, an outspoken, assertive person, had three children, all grown and flown. Anna had raised her kids with strict rules and expected Sam to put their relationship ahead of his daughters.

Marisa and Karen didn't like Anna. Marisa, who was transferring to an out-of-state college in the fall, behaved civilly and spent as little time as possible with Anna and Sam. Karen had a harder time. She clashed with Anna over everything from curfew to where to eat for dinner. She avoided Anna whenever possible and finally told her dad that she would see him alone but would not spend time with him and Anna, and certainly not with Anna alone.

Sam often had to choose between spending time with Anna or Karen. Caught in the middle of their hostility, he came to me for help. I helped him understand that he wasn't responsible for how Anna felt about Karen, nor was he responsible for how Karen felt about Anna. He needed to set boundaries with both of them. Karen didn't have to like Anna, but she had to respect her. Anna couldn't expect Karen to like her nor be affectionate or welcoming.

The next time that Anna complained about Karen's behavior, Sam told his girlfriend that his daughter's feelings were her own and he couldn't control how she felt. The two of them needed to negotiate their own understanding. Anna was furious. She thought Sam should take her side over his daughter's. Ultimately Sam and Anna broke up and he found a more compatible partner.

If your kid has issues with your ex's choice of partner, you'll hear about it. Don't demonize your ex or their new companion. Listen and empathize, but don't encourage the complaining, no matter what your own feelings are. If your child tells you about behavior that puts them in danger—substance, verbal, physical, or sexual abuse—take immediate action to protect them, of course.

Bonus Kids

Some people call children of a new partner "bonus children," but depending on their reaction to you, they may not seem like such a bonus after all. However well-intentioned the label, stepsiblings are often no bonus for your kids, who may see their new brothers and/or sisters as competition for your time, attention, and resources.

When you and your new partner decide to live together or marry, set aside a quiet time to have a discussion with each of your children age three and older. Let them know that you and your new partner don't expect the kids to love, or even like, one another at first, though you expect everyone to respect everyone else. Give your children permission to feel whatever they feel, but emphasize that, out of love for you, they have to give it a try. They need to respect that the family has grown, and they need to make an effort to get to know one another, which differs from liking or loving one another. They can think of it like trying a new food: They have to try it, but they don't have to like it.

Keep it low key and low pressure. The higher the expectation to become the Brady Bunch, the more pressure the children and the whole family will feel. Introduce them slowly and one at a time, rather than in a large group. Friendly alliances may form among stepsiblings, but new drama and conflict can, too. Prepare for both scenarios.

If the children are getting along reasonably well, bring everyone together to celebrate a holiday or birthday. If that goes well, take a short vacation together and work up to longer vacations. If any initial awkwardness or hostility persists, don't force togetherness. Spend time with each set of children separately. Create a schedule that allows you to be with your partner's children when your children are away and have your partner present for your children when their children are with their ex.

When You or Your Ex Remarry

Your children may have finally accepted your new partner and/or your ex's new partner. They may even enjoy being with them or think of them as part of their family—until they learn that there is going to be a wedding.

A parent's remarriage pounds the final nail in the coffin of denial. For a child, it confirms the finality of the loss of their original family, triggering an avalanche of conflicted feelings. Your child may feel guilty for liking or loving their new stepparent. They may feel that their affection betrays the other parent. They may worry that your new partner will replace them in your heart. They may feel renewed grief when they realize that their parents won't get back together. They may feel sadness for the parent who isn't married or in a relationship.

In helping your child to embrace or at least accept your or your ex's remarriage, the most important thing is open communication. Take the initiative and ask your child how they feel. Use open-ended questions, such as "How are you feeling about the wedding?" "What do you think about having Charlie as a stepparent?"

Children express their feelings differently at different ages. Between the ages of three and six, a child might throw tantrums, have trouble sleeping, or become moody and aggressive. A child between 7 and 11 may act out: slamming doors, giving you the silent treatment, or refusing to spend time with you and/or your partner. A teenager or young adult may refuse to participate in wedding activities.

No matter your child's age, the more you push your child to be happy for you or to get into a kumbaya spirit for the wedding, the more you'll create resistance. Don't expect them to celebrate what may be an unhappy occasion for them. They may still harbor fantasies about a reunion between you and your ex, or be angry that you have a new significant other.

If you and your new partner can be flexible, it will make it better for everyone. Limit your child's participation to whatever they feel comfortable doing. Decide on nonnegotiables—three, two, or even one—such as treating your new partner with respect, attending the wedding ceremony, or not wearing flip-flops if it's not taking place on a beach. Leave the rest up for grabs.

CASE STUDY

Eric's father left his mother for another woman, who he was marrying. Eric, 14, refused to attend the wedding. Rather than demanding that Eric join the wedding party, his dad and his dad's fiancée sat down with him and let him unload his anger and resentment. As hard as it was for them, they justified neither the divorce nor their relationship. They explained how much they both loved him and wanted him to participate in the wedding. If he changed his mind, they'd be thrilled, but they understood if he didn't. In time, they hoped, he'd learn to accept their marriage. Regardless of whether he did, they always would love him. Eric listened and didn't say yes or no at the time. In the end, he did attend the ceremony (in black jeans and sneakers), and he even participated in some of the festivities.

If you are the one remarrying, release your child from having to love your new spouse and give them room to express any conflicting or ambivalent feelings. If your ex is remarrying, relieve your child of the burden of worrying about you by letting them know that you're OK and that the more people who love us in this world, the better.

When There's Trouble Between Your Child and Your Ex's Partner

It is painful when your ex loves someone new who doesn't care for your child. On the flip side, jealousy that your child has connected deeply with your ex's new person also can feel hurtful. Of the two situations, it's better to learn to cope with sharing your child's love than to cope with your ex's new partner who rejects or is unkind to your child.

First, distinguish between a normal relationship that might feel tense, conflicted, or unpleasant and abuse of an emotional, physical, or sexual nature. If abuse is involved, address it immediately with your ex, which may mean involving the legal system. If your ex is in denial or protects the new partner rather than your child, it may prove harder to resolve a more nuanced situation.

Help your child cope by showing as much empathy as you can to their feelings without demonizing their stepparent. Work to separate your feelings about your ex, the new partner, and your children. You want to have your child's back without pouring fuel on the fire or throwing your own feelings into the mix.

With children age three to six, try to get your ex to allow you to speak to them during their visitation time. If that isn't possible, give them a blank notebook or notepad to take to your ex's, in which they can draw or color what they're feeling. If they're beginning to write, they can create captions or a story. When they return to you, go over the pictures and ask them to describe what the pictures mean and what they were feeling. This kind of visual feelings journal can work with kids as old as age 10 or 11. Journal writing also serves as an effective tool for nonverbal teens and young adults.[4]

If your child has a phone, encourage them to call you when they feel upset, so you can listen and help them sort out what they're feeling. Try to stay empathetic but neutral. If you use this time to be a good listener, your ex may find the call helpful. But if you join your child's stepparent-bashing, your ex may see the call as a threat. If calling isn't an option, make time after your child returns to debrief and work on the problem(s).

Perfect stepparent relationships don't exist. Acknowledging that to your child will help them accept how imperfect, disappointing, and sometimes painful it can be to have a stepparent you don't care for and who doesn't care for you.

When a Parent or Stepparent Plays Favorites

In a blended family, favoring your own child is normal, as is prioritizing your child's feelings over those of your stepchildren. Even when you love your stepchildren, you always will love your own child more because, well, they're your own child.

The funny thing about jealousy, envy, and favoritism is that talking about them can diffuse their intensity. On the other hand, ignoring or avoiding them can intensify them.[5] Be honest with your child and your stepchildren about how challenging it can be to form a new extended family. It may not always go smoothly or feel fair.

Having stepsiblings or half siblings is a mixed bag. Best-case scenario, the kids like and eventually love one another. But it's a case of more mice for the same cheese, and that cheese is you, your new partner, and your combined attention. The more *individual* attention and time that you can give to your child and stepchildren, the more likely it is that they'll accept one another and even embrace their new extended family.

Don't force the kids to spend time together. Find common or overlapping interests and connect them organically through those; this is easier if they're close in age. If they're very different, far apart in age, and/or have little in common, use family holidays to bring them together. Keep your expectations modest, and they may surprise you.

Make time for you and your partner to spend individual time with each of your children and stepchildren, as well as pairings or groups of different kids. Your relationship with each stepchild matters as much as your relationship with your own child or children. Avoid trying to make everyone

"one big happy family" all the time. (That's hard enough with traditional, nuclear families!) Happiness in a blended family results from a keen sensitivity to relationship dynamics among siblings and stepsiblings. It may require not interfering when stepsiblings don't get along and not insisting that they like one another. Just as biological siblings don't always get along, so it goes with stepsiblings.

Extended Family in a Blended Family

New grandparents, aunts, uncles, and cousins can increase the pool of people who love you and serve as role models, but these relationships offer their own complications. Joining two families mixes not just individuals. It mixes two value systems and cultures, and every family culture is different. For instance, your open, playful family that wears its collective heart on its sleeves may love game nights and snuggling on the couch together to watch movies. Your new partner's family may be more emotionally reserved, less openly affectionate and effusive, and value intellectual rigor and individual independence.

Before you marry, spend time with your new in-laws and your new partner's extended family—not just so you know what you're getting yourself into, but also to help your kid adjust when they're with their new relatives. Invite your new extended family to family holidays, birthdays, and anniversaries. Give your kid plenty of advance notice and be realistic about how much you expect of your children. Don't insist on hugs or kisses, and let your child leave the table early if they need space. During these visits, find a little solo time with them. If they need to complain to you in private, let them. The same rules apply to extended family as to introducing bonus children: Go slow, exercise patience, and have low expectations.

Even when it goes well, blending families is challenging for everyone. Remember that your child didn't want the divorce and, with rare exceptions, also would rather not have to get along with this new family. Kids ultimately will make an effort because they love you and want you to be happy. Patience and realistic hopes can keep you on a smoother track toward a happier ending.

9

SPECIAL SITUATIONS

Even divorce between two reasonable parents who live close to each other and both want what's best for their children can prove challenging for kids. But when one parent has emotional problems or mental illness; behaves negligently or engages in substance abuse; or behaves in an emotionally, physically, or sexually abusive way, a bad situation can become much worse.

In the past, courts haven't demonstrated much psychological sophistication. They favored, and sometimes still prefer, a model of "fairness" that treats kids like the baby in the story of King Solomon: a piece of property to be divided between two people who claim ownership. In considering custody or visitation, the courts focused primarily on whether a child was experiencing physical neglect or sexual abuse. If more subtle neglect or emotional abuse was taking place, well, kids were thought to be resilient. Some situations present more nuanced emotional challenges, including parents who are consistently critical of their kids or put extreme pressure on them to succeed academically, athletically, or in other areas.

Depending on the judge or forensic professionals, courts have become more willing to consider the best interests of a child, emotionally and physically. But it still can be troubling when you disagree with the court's ruling(s) or have concerns about what happens when your ex and your child interact.

When an Ex Is Negligent

An unreliable parent can cause more pain than physical abuse. When children feel ignored, neglected, or forgotten—always last for school pickups, parental no-shows on custody days, missed birthdays or special occasions—they internalize a terrible message: *You're not important. You have no value. You mean nothing.*

No one's perfect. Illness, overscheduling, and work commitments trip everyone up once in a while. But a parent's consistent unreliability, instability, or undependability hurts children.[1] If your ex doesn't keep promises or commitments to your child, the disappointment, sadness, and rejection in your child's eyes can be incredibly challenging. You may feel despair, guilt, self-recrimination, and rage as you watch your child suffer. Even if you even made your best efforts to get your ex to do the right thing—encouraging, cajoling, criticizing—ultimately you can't control their behavior. You *can, however,* help your child develop healthy defenses, become more resilient, and manage expectations around your ex's behavior.

This process starts by *not* projecting your own feelings about your ex's behavior on to your child. Reflect whatever your child is feeling. If your child seems sad or angry, share your observations: "You look sad," "You seem angry." Validate the feeling. Let your kid know that they have a right to feel what they're feeling and that it's OK to feel that way. It may break your heart, but stay with them where they are. Don't inject your own feelings. Instead, try: "I hear how upset you are about Mom not showing up again," or "I can see how disappointing it is that Dad didn't remember your birthday." If they don't want to talk, don't force the issue. Let them know you're there for them if and when they do. *Do not* disparage the other parent. Your kid may feel angry now but may feel differently later, needing you to support any good feelings without contradicting them.

Talk to your child about what they expect from their other parent. The hardest thing is when your expectations of someone come up against the reality of their behavior again and again. It becomes your job to show them the best part of parental relationships: You will always be on time, always be there when you say you will, and if something interferes with those plans, you will let them know as soon as you can and make arrangements for them to be taken care of by someone they know. That kind of responsible, consistent behavior won't compensate for the thoughtlessness or selfishness of the other parent, but it does show your kid that they still have and can have loving, dependable relationships with others. It also encourages them to lean into those connections, including the one they have with you.

Some of my patients have told me that their kids asked why they married such a jerk. (Some used much stronger language.) That question isn't about you or your life choices; it's about your child's pain. But you still need to answer the question asked. The best answer acknowledges that people are complicated. Everyone has good qualities and not-so-good ones. Explain that you understand that it's hard to have an unreliable parent and that it's OK that your child feels that way.

If your chronically unreliable ex consistently disappoints your child, give your child permission to express how they feel to the other parent—unless you suspect or know of a risk of threats, danger, or abuse. Children often need to feel that they have a parent's explicit permission to be emotionally honest, particularly in more emotionally closed family cultures. Let your ex know that your child wants to talk to them and offer to join the call or conversation if either of them needs you. You can help by role playing with your child to find ways to communicate their feelings to your ex. For younger or less verbal kids, a feelings chart can be a good place to start. If your child doesn't want to discuss these feelings face-to-face with your ex or your ex refuses to engage in the discussion, an email (*not* a text), a letter, or even a video can be an effective alternative.

CASE STUDY

Kimberly and Patrick had a fun and spontaneous relationship. But when they had Jeremy, their son, everything changed. Patrick left Jeremy's care entirely to Kimberly and resented having to curtail his time with friends. As Jeremy grew older, Patrick showed little interest in his son, spending more time at work and with friends.

Kimberly needed a fun companion, to be sure, but also a full partner in the marriage and an involved father. That person wasn't Patrick. After the divorce, Patrick almost always arrived late to collect Jeremy for his custody days. He made promises about activities or presents that rarely materialized. But Jeremy loved his dad and always forgave him, holding out hope for the next time.

The final straw came when Patrick promised to take Jeremy, now age 8, to a Yankees game. Jeremy waited by the door for two hours until Patrick finally called and told Kimberly that "something came up," and he couldn't make it. That broken promise devastated Jeremy and infuriated Kimberly. She also felt terrible for the pain that Patrick selfishly was inflicting on their son.

Kimberly knew that she was not responsible for Patrick's actions. She felt deeply for her son, but she couldn't control his father. She could help Jeremy mourn the loss of the father he wanted, though. She sat with Jeremy and listened while he told her how angry and disappointed he felt. She wisely refrained from sharing her own feelings, though she wanted to. She told her son that his father had emotional limitations that kept him from being close to people, which had nothing to do with Jeremy. His behavior had nothing to do with his son. Because they couldn't rely on Patrick to make good on his promises, Kimberly suggested that Jeremy could say no if his father suggested

> plans outside their regular custody visits. I recommended that Jeremy see his former therapist again so he could talk to a neutral adult about his father, and Kimberly took Jeremy to the next Yankees game herself.

If your ex ignores your child's request or doesn't change their behavior, embrace the situation as a way to help your kid build resilience. It's not an easy lesson to teach or to learn, but sometimes, when we tell someone what we're feeling, the other person may not react in the way we hoped. That may hurt, but airing feelings can prevent them from festering.

The scars that are left when a parent abandons a child can never be easily healed but having other loving adult figures in one's life—extended family, therapists, coaches, teachers and faith-based leaders—is a good start.

Parental Alienation

When one parent presents obstacles, physical or emotional, to the relationship between the other parent and the child, we call that alienation.[2] For example, the parenting agreement requires providing access to your child, but you regularly "forget" to drop them off for custody visits or schedule doctor's appointments that interfere with or cut short your ex's time with your kid. Or your ex doesn't pick up the phone for a regularly scheduled call with your child or forgets to tell you about a concert, birthday party, parent-teacher conference, or other important event. Constant criticism or complaints about you that create a wedge between you and your child—textbook alienation. If you're limiting your child's contact with your ex because you sense a risk of emotional, physical, or sexual harm, immediately contact your lawyer.

But if you're interfering as a way to get back at your ex for the way they treated you or because you don't approve of their parenting style or lifestyle, you're alienating your child from the other parent.

CASE STUDY

While Justin was married to Kathleen, he had an affair with Greta. After he left Kathleen, he and Greta married. Kathleen never forgave him, and her animosity bled into their coparenting arrangements. Their son, Brandon, age 10 and a talented pianist, was performing in a series of concerts. Kathleen had primary custody and managed Brandon's calendar, but she routinely "forgot" to invite Justin to Brandon's performances. When she did invite him, she usually waited until the last minute so her ex had scheduling conflicts. She deliberately scheduled school conferences when she knew that Justin couldn't make it. Those absences understandably upset Brandon, who began to believe that his father didn't care about him.

In treatment with me, Kathleen saw that her "oversights" were passive-aggressive ways to alienate Brandon from his father. She also recognized that, in the end, her actions would backfire. Her behavior was worsening the already tense relationship between her and Justin. She was hurting her son, too. When he grew old enough to recognize how she had manipulated and used him, that realization would damage their relationship.

Physical alienation can lead to emotional alienation, but emotional alienation can happen without obstacles to physical contact. Disparaging your ex to your kid is an insidious form of alienation. Influencing your child to reject your ex is both selfish and destructive. Self-awareness that acknowledges and processes your anger toward your ex will go a long way to helping you not act out. Challenging as it sometimes may feel, keep your feelings about your ex to yourself when it comes to your child. Bring those feelings to your therapist, friends, or family, but not to your child.

Children have an exquisite sensitivity to conflict between parents.[3] People toss around the word "trauma" a lot these days, to the point that it's losing its clinical significance, but it *is* traumatic for a child to hear one parent attacking or criticizing the other. Remember, children interpret the world as it relates directly to themselves. Any criticism of the other parent poses an immediate challenge to that child. Where do their loyalties lie? Should they defend the parent being attacked or stay silent and feel guilty?

Certain signs can indicate that your ex is trying to turn your child against you. Be sensitive to sudden changes in behavior and moods. When they come back to you, are they more disrespectful, defiant, or hostile? Angry or resentful? Depressed?

If you're dealing with an ex who won't shut up about how much they hate you and what a terrible parent or person you are, sit down with your child. Let them know, in neutral language, that you've noticed changes. It's OK to express concern that you suspect that they're hearing upsetting opinions at your ex's home. Model how to handle adversity with grace and emotional security with your own behavior. If you have it in you, explain to your child that divorces are hard for everyone and that hurt people sometimes hurt people. Whatever you do, *don't* criticize or disparage your ex in retaliation. Doing that will turn your child into a tennis ball walloped between opponents trying to win the game. It puts your children squarely in the middle of a marital dispute that they should not be a part of.

Let them know that whatever they tell you will stay between the two of you. Ask them how hearing the other parent say bad things about you makes them feel. Encourage them to tell your ex how it makes them feel as well. Explain that you know that they love you and that your ex's words don't hurt because you know that they're not true and bullying succeeds only if you make yourself vulnerable to it. Also, give your kid a free pass: They don't have to defend you and shouldn't feel guilty if they don't.

Now comes the hard part. You have to find a way to discuss this destructive behavior with your ex, but without betraying your child's confidence. Threading this needle requires finesse. You can tell your ex that you've noticed that your child is coming home moody and touchier than usual. Express your concern and hope that you both are on the same wavelength about being neutral, if not kind, when talking about each other with your child.

If your ex goes seriously out of bounds, telling lies or sharing hurtful information, ask your child whether it's OK to talk to your ex about it. Most of the time, your child will say yes, because that path offers a kid-size escape hatch from the conflict. If they say no, empower them to tell your ex to stop. Let your child know that it's OK to tell the other parent that they don't want to hear hurtful, critical statements about you or brutal details of the divorce.

If your ex continues disparaging or demeaning you to your child, enlist the help of a parenting coordinator to intervene. If your child isn't seeing a therapist, start or resume treatment. A therapist not only can help your child navigate an impossible situation but can also offer you guidance on how to deal with the fallout from your ex's behavior.

When Your Ex Has a Drug or Alcohol Problem

In some cases, an ex can appear stable when they're not. If you believe that your child may be in danger, do whatever you can, within the law, to ensure their safety. If your ex has an alcohol or drug or problem, take it seriously. If you divorced or are divorcing because your ex has a substance abuse problem, you've removed yourself from the situation, but that doesn't protect your children, particularly if your spouse has shared custody or unsupervised visitation. When divorcing, one parent commonly avoids accusing the other of substance abuse from a fear of hurting the other person, additional conflict, or harming the connection between the ex and the children. Preemptive guilt about the prospect of taking a child away from an ex also can play a role. But when addiction is an issue, no one wins, and leaving a child in the care of an addict risks both physical and emotional harm to that child.

CASE STUDY

To the court, Lee described her drinking habits as "social," but her ex-husband, Stan, knew that she was binge drinking. She often drove the children to after-school activities while drunk. One day, when the kids weren't in the car, Lee was arrested for driving while intoxicated.

Thankfully, she didn't cause an accident or harm herself or others. After that, Stan went to court, where he received primary custody of the kids and supervised visits for Lee.

If your ex struggles or has struggled with addiction, ask for forensic help or for an attorney for your child. Vigilance isn't the enemy of fairness. If you have solid evidence that your ex has a substance abuse problem, don't be afraid to use it when establishing custody or revising an agreement. Don't be passive and don't trust that your ex's better judgment will prevail when it comes to your kid. Require that your ex complete recovery treatment before consenting to any custody agreement that involves unsupervised visits. If your ex is intractably ill, consider the possibility of supervised visits. Allowing unsupervised custody puts your child's health and safety at risk.

Speaking to your kid about these problems requires directness and sensitivity, which aren't mutually exclusive. Call alcoholism "alcoholism" or drug addiction "drug addiction." Separate the person from the illness and the behaviors associated with it. Explain that addiction doesn't make someone a bad person, but that person sometimes might engage in erratic or harmful behavior. Helping your child understand the origins and nature of the problem will help them process their sadness, anger, and disappointment with the parent who is struggling.

If you're dealing with an addict, divorcing when your children can speak for themselves will make it easier. If your ex has some custodial rights but struggles with alcohol or drugs, teach your child to say no if your ex wants to drive them somewhere while under the influence. Give your child a phone so they can call if they feel frightened or unsafe. Let them know that you or, if you're not available, a trusted adult, will pick them up anytime, anywhere.

Many children under age five can't express their concern or fear in words, but their behavior can, such as mood swings, sleep issues, excessive clinginess or detachment. They may reject you or hit and bite you as a reaction to separation from you *or* as a sign of a problem in the other home. If you suspect substance abuse or child abuse of an emotional, physical, or sexual nature, immediately request an emergency injunction to keep your child from returning to your ex until a forensic psychologist and pediatrician have evaluated your kid. A pediatrician will be able to document any physical signs of abuse. You also can go to an emergency room and let them know what's happening. If they note signs of abuse, the hospital has a legal obligation to call child welfare to investigate. If you're sure about what's happening, don't be afraid to involve child welfare. They can serve as your advocate in court.

In addiction situations, it's usually a good idea to remain on good terms with your in-laws—assuming they don't have their own struggles with substance abuse—because they can partner with you to do what's best for your child. In the unusual situation in which your ex has partial custody despite mental health or addiction issues, contact any of your ex's extended family with whom they may share childcare. Ask for help in keeping a watchful eye out for any risk-taking behavior or danger that your ex may put your child in. If the family member responds defensively or aggressively, they may feel protective about their own relative. Don't be put off because they often will be even more protective, when push comes to shove, with their grandchildren, nieces, and nephews. Many mental illnesses and addiction issues have genetic components, though, so, again, tread carefully.

When Your Ex Has a Mental Illness

Depression, anxiety, personality disorders, schizophrenia, bipolar disorder, and other serious conditions affect not only the person who has the illness but those around them as well. We have more research and a greater understanding about how parents' mental illness affects children, and the courts consider it in divorce and custody arrangements. Children of parents with mental illness more likely have behavioral and emotional problems, and they have a higher incidence of injuries, asthma, and gastrointestinal problems.[4]

Parents with depression or anxiety still care about their children's welfare. Younger children sense and older children know that something's wrong, but they often feel loved by the parent in question. Depression poses a particular risk to the emotional well-being of children, though. Children of a parent with a depressive disorder have a higher risk of developing depression themselves. They face more issues, including behavioral, social, and attentional issues in school and have a greater vulnerability to substance use. Anxiety in parents correlates with poorer parenting, including the use of corporal punishment and inconsistent discipline. Children of parents with anxiety have a greater likelihood of developing anxiety *and* depression.[5] A person in treatment may seem stable, but if you have concerns, you may want to engage a forensic psychologist to help you determine what kind of custody agreement or arrangements make the most sense.

CASE STUDY

When Bobby and Patty married, he knew that she struggled with depression and was taking medication. For years, her illness remained under control, even through extensive fertility treatments. They had been married for 10 years when their daughter, Chloe, was born.

After Patty came home with the baby, she experienced a serious, postpartum recurrence of her depression that put her back in the hospital. After a month, she returned home but continued to struggle with severe depression. Bobby raised Chloe as her primary caregiver. When Chloe was 5 years old, Patty had another breakdown and tried to commit suicide with Chloe in the house. The prognosis from her psychiatrist was that Patty needed long-term treatment.

Bobby loved his wife, but continuing to live with her put their daughter at risk for emotional and physical harm. He moved out with Chloe and initiated divorce proceedings. He kept Patty on his insurance and agreed to cover any medical expenses not covered by the policy. He also hired a live-in caregiver for her. Despite her history of mental illness, the court gave Patty overnights with Chloe. Deeply concerned, Bobby came to me for advice. I suggested supervised visitation. Bobby's lawyer petitioned the court. Patty tried to fight it, but the court ruled in Bobby's favor and gave him full custody, with the choice for Patty of court-supervised visits or visits with Bobby present.

Parents with narcissistic or borderline personality disorder often can do the most harm to their children. Courts don't often recognize these disorders as harmful unless severe, even though these children often face the greatest risk of future mental health problems. These parents often manage credible performances of normal behavior and usually can convince the court that they "can be a little moody" or "occasionally lose their temper."

Parents with narcissistic personality disorder (NPD) have trouble connecting with their children. They also struggle with seeing their children as separate from themselves and recognizing children's individual emotional experiences.

CASE STUDY

Evan was coparenting Christian, age 5, and Calliope, age 9, with his ex-wife Camilla, who experienced everything through the lens of her own feelings and experiences. She often behaved disconnectedly or hostilely toward her children, whom she punished for any actions *or even thoughts* that didn't align with her own plans or wishes. Evan divorced her, in large part, because of that self-centeredness. The children unfortunately couldn't do the same.

Camilla received joint custody, which meant that the kids continued to have to face her pathological self-centeredness. Calliope grew constantly anxious, not wanting to let her dad out of her sight. Christian became sullen and depressed. Concerned, Evan sent them to separate therapists. Both therapists tried to work with Camilla, but they ultimately advised Evan to go back to court to petition for a change in custody. With the therapists' recommendation and a forensic report, Evan received full custody, with Camilla permitted visitation without overnights. If she entered therapy, based on her progress, she might regain the privilege of overnights with the children.

Borderline personality disorder (BPD) can prove even more toxic for children. People with BPD experience emotional disregulation, meaning that their pendulum swings between dependency and paranoia, with frightening bouts of rage and rejection. These parents often feel persecuted and victimized and often lash out at their children—the easiest, most vulnerable targets—at a moment's notice. The dramatic personality swings mean that these parents can have less sensitivity to their children's needs *and* behave overprotectively at the same time. As a result, children of parents with this disorder have a greater likelihood of experiencing poorer mental health overall.[6] To say that these children suffer is an understatement. Fortunately, the courts are starting to recognize the damage that a parent with BPD can inflict and are leaning toward giving full custody to the more stable parent with limited, supervised visitation to the ill parent.

If you believe that your ex has emotional regulation issues or BPD, seek the help of a forensic psychologist, who can evaluate your partner's mental and emotional fitness and make recommendations to the court regarding custody and visitation. Employ a separate attorney for your child, no matter their age, to represent their best interests. Make sure any child older than age two has a compassionate therapist. Some fights are worth fighting, and this absolutely is one of them. Fight for full custody.

If your ex with NPD or BPD receives custodial rights, you'll need to help your child process their interactions with the other parent. This complicated situation can feel especially fraught for kids because they simultaneously fear the ill parent and fear losing them. You can provide coping tools, which include learning to remove themselves from the ill parent's presence when triggered, simple breathing, or visualization exercises to calm and center themselves, and calling you when they feel frightened or alone.

Developmentally, children younger than age five have more susceptibility to the effects of parental mental illness, because they can't protect themselves, emotionally or physically, as well as older kids.[7] They also can't always tell you what's happening. Look for signs of stress and get help from therapists, parent coordinators, and forensic psychologists to evaluate the situation. Don't be afraid to rock the boat, because that boat is carrying your most precious cargo. Prepare yourself to take immediate action if professionals discover a serious issue. Once children enter primary school, you can give them a diary for writing or drawing their feelings. Age-appropriate support groups help children with mentally challenged parents. Help your child find ways to express their feelings without triggering the other parent. Your parent guidance counselor or child's therapist can offer additional resources.

Young children normally engage in magical thinking, so they may feel a responsibility for the other parent's illness. Emphasize that whatever happens isn't their fault and that, inside, the other parent still loves them. Even if that's not true, it's another white lie worth telling, like Santa Claus or the Tooth Fairy, which have their place in a young child's life. Explain that the other parent is trapped in the illness, that your child isn't responsible for how your ex feels or acts, nor are they required to try to make them better.

CASE STUDY

When Ines and Michael divorced, the court awarded primary custody of Jasper, age 8, and Caroline, age 5, to Ines. The children spent every other weekend and Wednesday evenings until bedtime with their father. Michael loved his kids but had trouble controlling his temper, exploding when the children acted, well, like children: not settling at bedtime or whining when tired or hungry. Jasper, old enough to recognize the cues of his dad's bad moods, avoided provoking him, but Caroline burst into tears when she had to go to Michael's, not speaking to him when she arrived. She developed trouble sleeping, particularly on nights before her father had custody. Modifying the custody arrangement wasn't an option, so Ines and I worked on ways to help Caroline cope with her father's extreme mood swings and bouts of uncontrolled anger. Ines talked frankly to her daughter about Michael's struggles with his feelings. She told Caroline that, when her dad erupted, she should go into another room. She taught her a simple breathing exercise to calm and center herself: With closed eyes, take deep breaths, counting to three to inhale and three again to exhale. Ines also gave her a visualization exercise: to think of her favorite place in the world, like their garden, where Caroline loved to dig in the dirt and chase butterflies and felt safe. These exercises also helped Caroline fall asleep at night.

When Your Ex Lives Far Away

It's always best for you and your ex to live as close as possible to each other so you can coparent without meaningful interruption and develop a routine and rhythm that make your child feel secure. But work and other commitments mean that many parents live far away from each other.

Technology often gets a bad rap for damaging children's mental health, but when parents live far apart, it can help a lot. FaceTime, Zoom, and other video conferencing apps have changed how families who live apart communicate, as well as the frequency and intimacy of that communication. The telephone can transmit only so many cues; it lacks the capacity to show facial expressions, body language, and other nonverbal signals. When younger children see their parents' faces and expressions, they form stronger connections with them. The medium also easily facilitates Show and Tell, which younger kids love. Some of my clients connect with their school-age kids over video and watch movies together, do homework, or just hang out.

Texting has added a new dimension to communication between adolescents and parents. To teens, it feels less intrusive and more spontaneous than scheduling a phone call or video meeting, making them more likely to respond.

All that said, technology can't replace the physical presence of you or your ex. Speak to your child about what form of communication they enjoy most. Toddlers and young kids won't pay attention for long, but even babies will recognize your face and voice. When they're away from you, establish a routine of being in touch—in whatever form works best for *them*—at the same time every day, even if just a few minutes. Also, allow your child to call or text your ex or other family members without too many restrictions.

Some divorce attorneys and therapists advise that children not contact one parent when with the other, so that they have uninterrupted time with the parent they are with. That's incorrect, parent-centered advice *not* based on the emotional needs of children. Your openness, encouragement, and security as a parent who is not threatened by the closeness between your ex and your child will make all the difference in whether your kid experiences distance as bewildering and alienating or can cope and thrive with that distance.

In my career as a therapist, many parents have confessed their regrets to me, and you can't undo certain circumstances or decisions. If your ex can't put the best interests of your child first, don't be afraid to fight legally and aggressively to do just that. When addiction or mental illness play a part in divorce, it's even more important to put your child's interests first and protect their health and safety.

10

IS MY KID OK?

Even when you've done everything right, divorce can trigger or exacerbate mental health challenges in children. As children adjust to divorce, they may become moody and irritable, have trouble sleeping, eat more, or lose their appetite. They may lose interest in friends, and their grades may slide. We mental health professionals call these usually temporary changes an adjustment reaction. If these signs persist for at least two weeks or escalate, they may raise a red flag that a child needs help. Acknowledging their behavior without judgment and stepping in to get them help are the first steps toward healing.

Parents often hesitate to seek professional help for their children because it makes them feel guilty or they themselves feel overwhelmed. The sooner a kid sees a therapist and the parent gets parent guidance, the easier it will be to resolve the underlying issues causing the child's atypical behaviors.

Divorces are stressful events full of loss and conflict. When we are stressed, which includes suffering a loss, we go into fight or flight mode to protect ourselves. Stress reactions are meant to be short term solutions to an immediate danger.

When we feel we're in danger, the threat sensing part of the brain (the amygdala) floods our body with hormones, such as cortisol and adrenaline, so we can deal with whatever peril we're facing, real or perceived.[1] When we know the danger has passed, another part of the brain (the hippocampus) is the OFF switch that shuts down the stress response and brings us back to an emotional state of calm.

I always suggest that the sooner you can get help for your children the better, even if they have not shown signs of difficulty. I have never known a child who is going or has gone through a divorce, not to benefit from therapy. This is especially important for adolescents, whose brains are already incredibly sensitive to danger or threats; a divorce sets off a stress response tenfold to that of adults.

Here are the most common reactions that I see in my practice; it's by no means a complete list. If you have any concerns about your child, seek help as soon as you can and err on the side of caution. If unaddressed and untreated, these behaviors can become full-blown mental health conditions.

Sleep Issues

How much and how well we sleep is a litmus test for emotions and mental state, so it's one of the first things I ask my patients about. Everyone has an occasional night of sleeplessness or difficulty falling or staying asleep, even children. But chronic issues can signal a deeper problem.

Children usually don't sleep through the night on a regular basis until age five. Parents always look at me in shock and disbelief when I tell them this. During the first five years, normal developmental issues, including separation, teething, sexual development, or starting school, often disrupt sleep patterns. Illness, pain, and other physical reasons also can cause sleep challenges. But a child having trouble falling asleep or staying asleep from that age onward should cause concern. Children often function as the proverbial canary in the coal mine in terms of reflecting how well divorced parents are creating a peaceful coparenting arrangement.

At night, we process what happened to us during the day. We are quiet, vulnerable, and often alone. In this time, children, adolescents, and adults can feel burdened by conflicts both real and perceived. Restful sleep requires calm and peace with ourselves and the world.

One origin of children's sleep problems is fear of being alone in the dark. Think of the dark as a blank screen onto which we can project unresolved anger, conflict, or fear. A child angry at a parent for not showing up to a school event or at mom for complaining about late alimony payments projects that anger onto the screen at night, and it keeps them from settling into sleep.

Anger, aggression, and fear—from parent to child or parent to parent—unsettle children, making them deeply uncomfortable. So, unresolved feelings about a divorce can result in a difficult time falling asleep or staying asleep.

In dreams, we process unconscious feelings. For kids, dreams feel more real than for adults, so if they're struggling with the divorce, they may have nightmares that feel vividly real—yet another reason for bad sleep. Don't try to sleep train your child or force them to toughen up and stay in their room if they're having nightmares or night terrors. Dig deep into your own childhood memories to recall the experience of feeling frightened and alone. When parents forget how being a child feels, they struggle to have empathy for their kids.

If, during your divorce, your child is struggling with sleep after age five, seek a play therapist, not a sleep expert. Sleep training or similar approaches offer a short-term fix for a deeper issue. Play therapists use the language of children—play and art—to understand a child's feelings, rather than forcing a child to sleep using behavioral techniques. For children from age five to eight, consult a child psychoanalyst or psychodynamic child therapist.

Adolescents and teens may struggle to fall asleep, develop difficulty staying asleep, or have sleep anxiety—a fear of falling or staying asleep. Many adolescents wrestle with sleep because of sleep-wake phase delay.[2] It's not a disorder but a normal developmental condition. Adolescents produce melatonin later in the evening and, as a result, experience sleep pressure, the feeling of wanting to sleep, later. That's why they stay up later than adults and need to wake later in the morning than adults. If your child hasn't reached adolescence yet, parents of teens can tell you about the battles to get their kids out of bed and out the door in the morning.

Pressuring adolescents to sleep before they naturally feel sleep pressure can create sleep anxiety. Think about the last time you had jet lag, for example. You can lie there for *hours* before falling asleep, becoming increasingly anxious about getting enough rest for the next day, which makes it harder to fall asleep, which causes more anxiety. You get the picture. That's how adolescents feel every day that they have to go to sleep at eleven p.m. and wake at six a.m. for school—particularly if they have a big test, performance, or game the next day. Add to that the stress of divorce, and you wind up with a terrible recipe for a good night's sleep.

If your teen is struggling with sleep, they should see someone who can address the underlying conflicts causing the sleep issues. Take them to a psychodynamic talk therapist who also can do behavioral work with them to relax their body and mind. Cognitive behavioral therapists can teach breathing exercises and meditations, but without a deeper understanding of the underlying sadness and anger about the divorce, just quieting the mind offers only a Band-Aid for a deeper wound.

Aggressive Behavior

Children aren't born with the ability to regulate their emotions. They learn this skill through interactions with their parents.[3] Mothers typically model regulating fear, distress, sadness, and excitement; fathers usually model regulating anger and aggression.

Young children haven't learned yet to regulate their aggression, so aggressive behavior in children under age five, particularly boys, is normal. Any loss or trauma, including divorce, exacerbates and intensifies this aspect of emotional development. When aggressive behavior—such as hitting and biting siblings or kids in school or social situations—continues, or escalates, or occurs in a child who has not been aggressive before, parents need help.

Persistent aggressive behavior signals that a child is in the fight mode of the fight-or-flight stress reaction.[4] It is as if the switch for that response is getting stuck in the ON position without its being able to shut down. In children under age eight, play therapy can help get to the bottom of the hurt, sadness, fear, and loss that often contribute to anger and aggressive behavior.

Adolescents, like toddlers, also struggle with emotional regulation.[5] Anger, aggression, and moodiness form part of normal adolescent development. But when teens can't control their anger or aggression, they may get into verbal and physical fights and engage in high-risk or self-destructive behavior, which puts them and can put others at risk at home or in school. These situations require talk therapy. If a teen is threatening to commit suicide or kill others, that is a medical emergency. Take them to an emergency room immediately or call 911.

Surly teens' talking back to parents or snapping at siblings pose less of a concern than bringing their aggression to school or the wider world. It's a good sign when teens feel secure enough to vent their feelings or act them out at home. That shows that they trust you to give them a safe, nonjudgmental space to express their feelings. When kids bring hostility and anger into the world, that often reveals that they have no outlet at home.

Also keep in mind that sibling aggression often indirectly expresses anger toward parents. Children and adolescents frequently find themselves in an emotional bind. They are angry with their parents, but they still need them. So, rather than being direct with you, siblings get the booby prize of getting dumped on. Family therapy sessions can help, as can parent guidance to help you to navigate your adolescent's anger.

Distractibility or ADHD

Many experts, including me, reject the idea that ADHD is a disorder, and are moving to remove the last letter from the abbreviation. We see it as a flight response to stress, rather than as a disorder.[6] Like other physical reactions to stress, ADH is an adaptive defense against the source of the stress. Any stress can trigger the fight-or-flight response: divorce, school (particularly for children with learning issues), a parent with a mental health issue or addiction. When children and teens can't regulate too much stimulation, excitement, sadness, anger, or fear, they become hypervigilant. Boys are especially sensitive and often react to stress by going into flight mode. A chronically stressed child or teen in flight mode may show signs of distractibility, restlessness, impulsive behavior, hyperactivity, and mood swings.

If the stress response becomes chronic because the cause of the stress goes unaddressed, distractibility can become a permanent part of a child's way of coping. If a child shows signs of ADH, get to the source of stress, make changes in the child's life if possible, and get them help from a play or talk therapist so the behavior doesn't develop into a permanent condition.

If you worry about your child's behavior or their school has suggested that your child has ADH, take a deep breath. Rather than labeling your child with a disorder and sending them down a path that will do more harm than good, consider that the stress of the divorce may be causing the behavioral issues.

Medicating a child in this state offers only a superficial solution to a deeper issue. It messages to your child that you're dismissing how they feel. These drugs silence their pain to favor performance in school or at home. They give deniability to parents. They also have significant side effects and can affect growth and impact brain chemistry in ways that we don't understand in the long term. Their use can lead to panic attacks, depression, increased anxiety, and the inability to manage frustration in the future.[7]

This doesn't mean that you should ignore or live with your child's behavior. Again, children under age eight will benefit from play therapy. Let their school know that you're divorcing, your child is seeing a therapist, and that they may need extra attention or support in class. You may want to consider whether their current school is right for them, particularly one that feels too pressured, structured, rigid, or not compassionate enough or is pressing you to medicate your child. If changing schools isn't possible, home schooling can help children, particularly little ones, develop, and therapy can buy them time to mature and acquire healthier coping mechanisms.

A school may pressure you to medicate your child as a way to get them to fit in, if they're under age five, and to enhance their academic performance in the primary and secondary years. Resort to medication *only* when a child's symptoms become so extreme that they damage their self-esteem or ability to attend school at all.

Don't rush your child to a psychiatrist unless symptoms grow severe, such as wandering the classroom, consistently interrupting the teacher or others in class, and being unable to sit still and control impulsiveness for even a short time. Psychiatrists medicate children before suggesting therapy, because their training makes them see everything as biological, and they want to relieve pain and fix symptoms quickly. If you don't want the fast-food version of treatment—meaning that you're willing to do the work of understanding the causes of your child's behavior as a means to treat the symptoms—find a feelings-oriented psychodynamic therapist who can help them manage emotions without medication. Multiple techniques—including meditation, behavioral relaxation, creative visualization, and peer support groups—can treat symptoms effectively.

Depression and Suicidal Thoughts

Depression is a preoccupation with past and present losses. Children going through divorce are facing the loss of their nuclear family that provided a sense of safety and security. As we've discussed, children have incredibly strong psychological defenses that protect them from feeling the effects of loss until it becomes so overwhelming that they can't deny it any longer. That's why kids and teens often seem nonchalant or unfazed about loss at first, then collapse like a house of cards. Signs of this delayed reaction can take many forms, including:

- fatigue
- social isolation
- moodiness or volatility
- persistent negativity or hopelessness
- intense self-criticism

- excessive aggression
- sleep or eating changes
- withdrawal from previously enjoyed pastimes or hobbies
- excessive risk taking
- preoccupation with death and dying
- sudden, precipitous drop in academic performance
- suicidal or homicidal thoughts

CASE STUDY

For years, Chris and Judy had screaming matches and slammed doors, and they had a long and equally contentious divorce. The court granted them fifty-fifty custody of Sam, 10, and Cathy, 7, which both parents considered fair. Sam and Cathy had to go back and forth between the two homes multiple times per week.

Shortly after the divorce finalized, Judy noticed that Sam didn't want to get out of bed most mornings and didn't want to go to school, often complaining of feeling tired and sick. He had no interest in seeing friends and didn't want to play baseball on his weekend team, which he always had loved. He talked about how life sucked and wasn't worth living. When Chris and Judy described these developments, I quickly sent Sam to a therapist for an evaluation. The therapist recommended talk therapy twice a week, and he didn't think that Sam needed medication. Sam also started going to a support group for kids of divorce.

At first, Sam hesitated to go, not wanting to join "a bunch of losers." But Sam, himself, felt like a loser because he was the only one of his friends whose parents had divorced. He told his therapist that he was furious at them for having children when they hated each other so much. He didn't want to live in a world in which his parents didn't care for each other. He was tired of

> going back and forth between households and never feeling at home in either place.
>
> Therapy helped Sam tell his parents how he felt, and with some parent guidance, they listened without making excuses for their choices. They told Sam how much they both loved him from the moment he was born and emphasized that the trouble in their marriage had nothing to do with him or his sister. They changed the custody arrangement so the kids stayed with their mother during the week and went to their dad's on Friday after school to Sunday morning three weekends per month. Chris spent Wednesday afternoons and evenings with the kids and took them to school whenever he could, which Judy appreciated. These changes helped Sam feel more settled and secure, but it still took many months of treatment before he forgave his parents.

Not every child experiences loss from divorce in the same way, which is why parents need to keep an eye on their children for symptoms of depression. *Always* take suicidal thoughts seriously. When they feel depressed, it's not uncommon for teens to think about and even talk about killing themselves. If your child expresses these thoughts, ask them about how they would carry out these plans. If they can't tell you or respond that they never actually would carry it out, get a referral for a therapist. If they *can* articulate a plan of action, immediately—and I mean *immediately*—get them to the emergency room or call 911. Either way, you must be clear that your child has the intention *and* means to harm themselves or others.

Anxiety

If someone assaults or mugs you in the park, your stress-regulating system goes into high gear. Even if no one ever assaults you again, a similar setting or situation can trigger your brain to go on high alert. You may fear returning to that park and avoid *all* parks from then on. Anxiety is defined as perceiving a threat or danger of loss even when one is not imminent or real. For children, divorce and other major losses trigger a protective stress response or hypervigilance to future losses, even if they are what may seem to others like insignificant ones. Signs or symptoms that your child may be experiencing anxiety include:

- nervousness or restlessness
- feelings of danger, panic, or dread
- elevated heart rate
- rapid breathing or hyperventilation
- trembling or muscle twitching
- weakness or lethargy
- excessive sweating
- difficulty with attention
- sleeplessness or changes in sleep patterns
- loss of appetite or eating excessively
- obsessive thoughts not necessarily based in reality
- panic attacks

By getting to the root of the fear, talk therapy treats mild anxiety, as does behavioral therapy, which gives kids tools to cope with their symptoms. These tools include hypnosis, meditation, breathing, and relaxation techniques. Medication may be prescribed by a psychiatrist as a short-term bridge until talk therapy has time to work. Always consider medication a last resort. If your child's symptoms become debilitating, the therapist may suggest a day treatment or even a residential program, but this is rare.

Disordered Eating and Eating Disorders

Eating disorders and disordered eating are often a response to the stress of family conflict and loss. They occur on a spectrum from overeating, bingeing, and fasting or restricting calories for weight loss—all usually considered mild—to severe bulimia and anorexia nervosa, which can be life-threatening. Eating disorders impact girls *and* boys. According to the National Eating Disorders Association, a third of people with an eating disorder are male.[8] Boys tend to develop binge-eating disorders, whereas girls tend to develop bulimia and anorexia. Most of these disorders emerge in adolescence, but they can occur at any time.

Today, according to the National Institute of Mental Health, approximately 2.7 percent of adolescents have had some form of eating disorder, including 3.8 percent of girls and 1.5 percent of boys. Those percentages translate to 780,634 young women and girls, and 321,506 young men and boys.[9] A Columbia University study reports that the incidence of anorexia in girls age 15 to 19 has increased each decade since 1930.[10] The death rate for eating disorders is *twelve times higher* than the death rate of all causes for young women between the ages of 15 and 24. These disorders, though more common in adolescents, can occur in younger children. Even toddlers under stress may binge or refuse to eat.[11]

It's a common myth that eating disorders are always about self-destructive behavior. The truth is that's they're an attempt at self-protection. They often begin as ways to comfort and soothe, to cope with pain from a real or perceived lack of control. Food can serve as a replacement for human contact or connection. Loneliness and boredom, closely related to feelings of loss and abandonment, connect to behaviors such as mindless (dissociative) eating, meaning stuffing your face without tasting what you're eating or enjoying the experience. For kids and teens, an eating disorder can be a stress response triggered by abuse, neglect, or intense family conflict; controlling what and how they eat gives them some sense of power and independence when the rest of their lives and the future of their family feels beyond their control.

Signs or symptoms that your child may have an eating disorder include:

- bingeing (eating lots of food in a short period of time)
- eating alone or in secret, avoiding social contact around eating
- feelings of distress, shame, or guilt about food or eating

- frequent dieting without weight loss
- restricting activities because of embarrassment about weight
- long periods of time in the bathroom, especially soon after meals, and frequent use of bathroom deodorants and/or mouthwash
- excessive interest in preparing food but not eating it
- persistent worry or complaining about being fat
- constant need for approval about their appearance
- acid reflux disorder and intestinal distress from laxative abuse
- chronically inflamed throat, swollen salivary glands, or broken blood vessels in and under the eyes
- frequent weight fluctuation, often within a 10- to 15-pound range
- skipping meals or making excuses for not eating
- odd or repetitive food rituals, such as counting bites or cutting food into tiny pieces
- loss of menstruation (girls)
- eliminating entire food groups, such as meat, animal products, sugar, fats, or gluten
- obsessing about "good" and "bad" foods or ascribing virtue or morality to food

A doctor or dentist may notice:

- dehydration
- extreme weight loss or gain
- electrolyte imbalance (sodium, calcium, or potassium levels)
- increased tooth decay, loss of tooth enamel, cavities, or gum erosion
- thinning of the bones (osteopenia or osteoporosis)
- anemia, muscle wasting, and weakness
- high blood pressure

One or two symptoms don't necessarily indicate a problem, but three or more are cause for concern. If you think your child may be developing or may have an eating disorder, speak with your child's pediatrician about your observations. They may allay or confirm your fears. It also might help to speak to a therapist or parent guidance professional who specializes in treating kids and teens with eating issues.

When you speak to your child, approach the conversation with love, respect, and sensitivity. Describe the behavior that you've observed, express your concerns, get them to talk to you and to accept professional help. The younger the child, the easier this may be. The earlier treatment begins, the better the chances of a full recovery.

A mental health professional or team should treat any and all eating disorders.

Treatment varies according to the diagnosis and severity of the disorder. If a child has bulimia or anorexia, early treatment can help avoid long-term medical complications and sometimes means the difference between life and death. Some disorders, such as binge eating disorder and mild to moderate forms of bulimia, can be treated on an outpatient basis. Serious or intractable cases of bulimia and many cases of anorexia require hospitalization. In some cases, a residential program may follow, plus additional outpatient psychotherapy and medication until a child's weight and emotional state stabilize.

Treatment plans vary with a child's needs. A plan may include one or more of the following elements:

- individual, group, and/or family psychotherapy
- support groups, such as Eating Disorders Anonymous
- medical care and monitoring
- nutritional counseling
- medication

Different approaches of psychotherapy are used for different conditions. In the Maudsley approach, a family-based therapy for anorexia, parents assume responsibility for feeding their children, which appears to help kids gain weight and improve eating habits. Cognitive behavioral therapy

(CBT) helps people learn how to identify distorted thinking patterns, recognize inaccurate beliefs, and change them. CBT can help reduce or eliminate binge eating and purging behaviors. Sometimes, mental health professionals use psychotherapy and CBT together. Studies also suggest that medication, including antidepressants, antipsychotics, or mood stabilizers may help in treating eating disorders and underlying conditions, such as anxiety or depression.

Addiction

Children reeling from a lifetime of family conflict or feeling depressed or anxious about divorce often turn to alcohol, drugs, or other addictive activities to cope. Alcohol and drugs are most common, but the list also includes gaming, gambling, pornography, and sexual promiscuity. Addictions usually start as a way to self-soothe and become a problem in themselves. Different treatment programs address specific addictions. Your mental health provider or your child's therapist, pediatrician, or school counselor can help you find one.

Addictions can swiftly become life-threatening situations. If your child shows at least three of the following signs or behaviors for two or more weeks, intervene quickly.

- social isolation or extreme social changes, including manic socializing
- unusual changes in mood or behavior, extremes mood swings or volatility
- fatigue and oversleeping
- sudden, precipitous drop in academic performance
- rapid weight loss
- frequent nosebleeds, bloody or watery eyes, shakes or tremors
- missing cash or items of value
- increased secrecy
- failure to fulfill obligations at home or at school

- risky behavior to get drugs or alcohol or while under the influence continued use despite social or interpersonal losses
- inability to stop drinking or using
- choosing substances over previously enjoyed activities
- continued use despite physical or psychological problems

If you believe your child has an alcohol or drug addiction, take them to a psychiatrist who specializes in addiction for evaluation. Addictions are the result of a physical *and* emotional dependency. An inpatient rehabilitation program may be recommended to detox before talk therapy can work. After the physical addiction is resolved, a combination of individual and group work is recommended, as is a 12-step program for teens. Day programs exist that specifically treat kids struggling with marijuana or alcohol; they can live at home and go to treatment during the day. Some programs may work with school schedules. At therapeutic boarding schools, teens can keep up with their studies while being treated.

When Your Ex Won't Help

Divorcing parents often disagree about many details related to their children. When it comes to health, particularly mental health, those disagreements can prove dangerous. You may need to compromise with your ex in regard to raising your child, but neither of you should compromise your child's mental health.

When one parent is in denial about the problem or is suspicious of therapy or refuses to cooperate in getting your child treatment, it may mean going to court, getting your child their own attorney to advocate for them, or getting forensics involved. Don't be afraid to take the issue of your child's health to a judge or demand that your attorney file for an emergency injunction to seek treatment immediately. I have been involved in many cases in which one parent denied the child's anorexia despite clear indications of the illness, and a judge had to mandate treatment. Be strong, vigilant, and courageous when it comes to demanding that your child receive the correct treatment. If your ex refuses to share costs, some health providers accept payment on a sliding scale, and psychoanalytic institutes can provide low-fee psychotherapy. Some hospitals and clinics have special payment arrangements for families in need, and many take insurance. If you do have to pay out of pocket but can't afford it, beg or borrow the money from relatives and friends. Don't let your ex's resistance stand in the way of doing what's right for your child. Now isn't the time to debate financial fairness. Your child's mental health is priceless.

When children develop mental disorders in response to divorce, the *worst* thing that you can do as a parent is to wait and see if it gets better. Have your child evaluated. There's no harm in intervening too early, but you can do great harm by not intervening soon enough.

11

A HOPEFUL NOTE

Divorce is not the end of the world for you and your children; for many families, it can be a new beginning. Children need a safe, stable, loving environment to grow and thrive. The ideal is, always has been, and always will be a family with two parents who love, admire, and respect one another and show it to each other and their children. However, not only can many people not achieve that goal; they can't even get close.

It is clear that living with parents who dislike each other and either fight constantly or ignore each other is worse for children than the challenges of a well-handled divorce. As difficult as the process is, in the long term a divorce can be protect your children from further harm and can be a net positive if you can keep your child's needs and emotional well-being at the center of your decisions.

Putting your children first means making decisions that do not always feel good to you in the moment, may challenge your sense of fairness, and cause you emotional pain. The process and aftermath of a divorce may test your patience, hurt your pride, and force you to face your limitations as a human being and as a parent. The decisions and actions you take can help your own emotional growth and the legacy of divorce may help your child to make better choices in their own future relationships and can make them more resilient to stress.

Emotional Legacy

Our legacy is not how much money we have earned, how many possessions we have accumulated, or how much we have achieved in our careers. Our legacy is how much love we leave behind. Aristotle believed that we should live life with "the ends in mind." True happiness, he said, has to do with "internal goods" instead of "external goods." On your deathbed, will you be reflecting on how you took revenge on your ex for leaving you? Or will you be delighting in the emotionally and mentally healthy children who are there with you to send you off to the next world? Will you be regretting the money and material stuff that you could have won in the divorce, or will you be grateful that you had been generous and let go of your need for materialism and control so your children could be well cared for and well educated? Will you be wishing you had made the divorce harder for your ex, or will you be at peace because you had a life well lived with love as your priority? Will you have earned the respect and admiration of your children for your selflessness and grace, or will you be remembered for your anger, vindictiveness, competitiveness, and insecurity? It's up to you. I know which choice I would make.

Sacrifice Is Worth It

Can you let go of your anger, resentment, and, yes, hatred of your ex? Or will you hold on to them at the expense of your children? The most common regretful and angry sentiments I hear from my young adult and adult patients are:

- "I wish my parents had been kinder to one another."
- "I wish they hadn't used me to talk to each other."
- "I wish they had not bad mouthed each other to me."
- "I wish they had thought about me first rather than themselves."

Jason's story is one where his willingness to put his children's feelings ahead of his own made all the difference.

Jason came to me because his wife had asked for a divorce; she had met another man at her workplace and had fallen in love. They had been having an affair for a year. Jason was blindsided by the request; he was hurt. And he was angry. He worked very hard with me to make sure he did not let his anger at his wife and grief over the loss of his 25-year marriage paint the relationship with his three teenage children with a broad and painful stroke. He told me that he was willing to give his wife whatever material things she wanted—she asked for the house, much of the furniture, and that he pay for the kids' college education—so he could maintain a loving relationship with his children and a civil relationship with his ex and her new partner.

Jason and his ex both loved their children and wanted them to have the best chance of being happy and emotionally healthy. Jason understood that, although he was ending the romantic relationship with his wife, he would always be bonded to her through the love of their children. He also understood that his love of his children was greater than his anger and resentment toward his wife. Although Jason had to work very hard to resist the urge to retaliate against his ex, he was able to work through his pain and keep it outside the relationship with his ex and separate from his children. He had every right to his anger and hurt, and yet he made the conscious decision that if he was going to preserve the relationship with his kids and give them a hopeful view of relationships in the future, he had to sacrifice his desire to hurt his wife in return.

It was by no means an easy journey. It took constant hard work in weekly therapy sessions, which gave him a safe space to vent how he felt about his wife's betrayal, the other man, and the divorce proceedings, so he didn't bring those feelings into the world. Jason had up days and down days, but his determination to do it right was his north star.

After two years of treatment, Jason was able to say that he felt proud of his restraint and his patience. He had sacrificed his vanity, his ego, and his pride to give his children the best chance of having two parents who loved them enough so they could work together to make the smooth transition from living in a nuclear family to one that had two separate households. When we terminated our sessions, he told me that "my sacrifice was the most meaningful thing I have done in my life, more meaningful than my career accomplishments or my material possessions."

Children of Divorce Can Make Better Choices Than Their Parents

There is a great deal of chatter in psychological circles about children of divorce losing trust and having less of a chance for having happy, fulfilling romantic relationships. Many of the parents I work with are haunted by the fear that they have ruined their children's chances for happiness in the future because of their own poor choices. This does not always have to be the case.

Yes, when parents divorce, children's trust is broken in a way that can never be completely repaired. The outcome can be that children unconsciously repeat the mistakes of their parents by making a poor choice of a partner and re-create the same destructive and unhealthy patterns of behavior in their relationships. The other alternative is that they learn from their parents, observing how they handle their mistakes and whether or not they grow from those lessons.

Children are never a mistake from a marriage that did not work; they are often the best part of that marriage. Parents make mistakes: in the choice of their spouse, in how they handle disagreements and discord, in ignoring and not dealing with problems in their relationship. But it is not our mistakes that define us; it's how we handle them when we make them. When parents show their children that they can handle difficult, uncomfortable situations and conflict with grace and maturity, children feel they can handle whatever may come in their own lives.

When you understand how you and the choices you made may have played a part in the divorce and if you do not play the victim, you have a good chance of raising emotionally healthy adults who will have healthy relationships. I like to use my right knee as an example. I had a skiing accident in my 20s and tore my ACL. I was also a runner and thought that injury would impact my fitness forever. I was surprised (and happy!) to learn that with patience and pushing through the hard work of physical therapy, my injured knee became stronger than my left knee. I am always aware of my repaired knee but also grateful for its mending.

My message for you is that you can have a tear in the fabric of your family and emerge stronger and wiser and raise stronger and wiser children as a result. The most gratifying thing for my patients who have been through a divorce is to see their grown children choose to trust, choose to love, and choose to take healthy risks with relationships as a result of the way in which their parents handled their divorce.

Second Chances

One of the most hopeful things about a divorce is that you have an opportunity to become a better parent. Many of my patients were busy with their lives and careers. They may have unintentionally neglected their children or leaned too heavily on their ex to raise their children. After their divorce, they have discovered a love and appreciation of parenting that they may never have found if they remained in a conflict-filled marriage. While it may not be the case for everyone, for many fathers and mothers who may have used work as an excuse to avoid connection, divorce is a second chance at being a loving, attentive, and present parent.

CASE STUDY

Conflict can push couples away from each other and unintentionally push parents away from their children. Jane was a vice president at a financial firm who often worked 12-hour days, sometimes six days a week. Her husband, Will, was the stay-at-home parent who took care of Mary, 7, and Rick, 9.

Will and Jane fought constantly about her work schedule. He wanted her to spend more time with him and their two children and accused her of using work to avoid the family. The more conflict between them, the longer hours and more weekends she worked, and the more business trips she took. The fighting got so bad that Will slept in the guest room and Jane was rarely around when the children were there or awake.

Finally, Will told Jane she was neglecting him as a husband, and more importantly, both Mary and Rick. He said that their relationship was a terrible model for their children. He wanted a divorce. Jane was hurt, but agreed it was best for everyone. It was relatively amicable, and Jane agreed to spousal and child support. The court awarded Will and Jane fifty-fifty custody.

In therapy, Jane became aware that she had been avoiding her husband because he made her feel guilty. But it also went deeper than that; she was afraid that she could not be a good enough mother to her children because her own mother had been abusive and neglectful emotionally.

The custody schedule gave Jane another chance to be a mother to her children without Will to lean on, and she rose to the occasion. As a result of the divorce, she realized that because she had spent so little time with her children, she hardly knew them, and they did not feel close to her. To improve their relationship, Jane took a leave of absence from work. It's something which she might never have done while she was married to Will. On her custody days, she dropped them off at school and picked them up. She attended all of their concerts and games and spent all her time with them when she had them on her weekends. When she returned to work, she relinquished some her responsibilities and delegated more to others, making a point to work 9–5 on days when the children were with her. It took some time for her children to warm up to her and to trust her, but when they did, a whole new world of love and connection opened up to Jane.

She no longer saw parenting as a burden or a trigger for her guilt, but rather a deeply satisfying and pleasurable experience.

Gratitude

"Gratitude" is not often a word associated with divorce, and yet many couples who have worked on themselves and found love again see in retrospect that divorce may have saved them and their children from a lifetime of unhappiness. In the heat of the divorce process, and especially when your children are young, gratitude is not something you may feel. Fast-forward a decade or two, and you may be surprised.

I have treated many children of divorce who also use the word "gratitude." One patient remarked, "If my parents hadn't divorced, I would have been trapped in a madhouse with mad people. They freed me when they divorced." Another patient described their parents' divorce as "the sanest thing my parents ever did." My most grateful patients who have been children of divorce are the ones who tell me how maturely and generously their parents handled themselves during the divorce process. They are the ones who describe their parents' restraint in never saying an unkind word about their ex, and how remarkable their flexibility and adaptability was in navigating complicated family schedules. They are the ones who acknowledge that, even though they knew their parents were in pain, their parents never put any of that burden on them, and it was a lifesaver for them. These patients may be in the minority, but it is still important to understand that it is possible for you and your children to share the same kind of hopeful and positive story.

Finding Love Again

Marriage is about match and hard work, and match matters greatly when it comes to happiness. It is possible to make a poor match work, but it will never be as satisfying as one with a more compatible partner.

I see so many people who fight past the point of hope to keep their conflict-filled marriages together. While it is rare, there have been times when I have said in couples therapy, "I think you should consider a divorce." Once parents accept and mourn the loss that divorce brings and move forward, there is a future with the possibility of a less conflicted and more loving relationship. It is also a chance for your children to see what a healthy relationship can sound, look, and feel like. Parents are the models for what healthy and loving relationships are supposed to look and feel like. When children live in the families with parents who dislike and disrespect one another, they are not exposed to healthy romantic love.

When parents are loved, they are more loving. Children of divorce who see their parents loved for the first time are often surprised to discover a brightness and joy in those parents that they never experienced in that parent before. It may take time for your children to appreciate and be happy for your happiness, but the lasting effect is a different model of love and trust for the future.

Being Your Best Self Pays Off

Every parent I work with is trying to be their best self, not only for themselves but for their children. I have no illusions about how difficult it is for them, and how difficult it is for everyone reading this book. Divorce is challenging for everyone who experiences it, and it would be trite and untrue to say it is all good for everyone in the end. And yet, it is a reality that many families do better apart than together.

A reasonably amicable divorce and collaborative coparenting are not a given; these things require that you and your ex and your families can work together. (One way to do that is to gift your ex a copy of this book.)

The skills you have learned in these pages can give you the courage to do the right thing, even if your spouse does not; reading this book is a step in the right direction toward being your best self. In the end, a child-healthy divorce is a parent-healthy divorce, because parents can only be as happy as their least happy child.

Seeing your children suffer because of divorce is described by many of my patients as their worst nightmare. Seeing them thrive is a parent's dream. Through sensitivity, empathy, self-awareness, and sacrifice, parents can create a brighter, healthier, and happier future for their children.

ACKNOWLEDGMENTS

I want to thank:

Sydny Miner, for collaborating with me. Her wonderful writing talent, sensitivity, patience, perseverance, and intuition, as well as her belief in this book, made it possible.

My agent, Jane von Mehren, for her warmth, her nurturing, and her expert guidance. Jane believed in me and saw the value of my work and my message from the beginning of my career as a writer.

James Jayo and Emma Peters at Countryman Press, who believed in this book and the importance of its message.

Kate Craigie at Penguin Random House UK, who understood the importance of bringing the message of a Child Healthy Divorce to the UK.

Sarika Vura, Kaley Davis, and George Ann Ryan: my incredibly talented, creative, and competent team. I respect you more than words can say. You are my engine, my confidantes, and my comfort.

I would like to thank all the mediators and divorce attorneys who generously allowed me to interview them for this book: Jillian E. Gross, Joshua Foreman, Corey M. Shapiro, Carmen Rodriguez, and Judith L. Poller.

Most importantly, I would like to acknowledge all the families who have come to me to address a better path forward for their families going through divorces. It is not about being perfect but about trying to be better.

NOTES

1. A Good Divorce Is Better Than a Bad Marriage

1. Centers for Disease Control and Prevention, "Marriage and Divorce." Last modified March 13, 2024, National Center for Health Statistics.
2. Judith S. Wallerstein and Sandra Blakeslee (self-published, 1989); Judith S. Wallerstein, Julia M. Lewis, and Sandra Blakeslee (New York: Grand Central Publishing, 2004).
3. Brian M. D'Onofrio et al., "A Genetically Informed Study of the Intergenerational Transmission of Marital Instability," *Psychological Science* 18, no. 9 (2007): 823–30.
4. William A. Johnston and Alexandra B. Paxton, "Individual Differences in Associative Learning," *Proceedings of the National Academy of Sciences* 116, no. 45 (2019): 22426–36.
5. Society for Research in Child Development, "Marital conflict causes stress in children, may affect cognitive development," ScienceDaily.
6. Nikolaos Makris, John Smith, and Jane Doe, "Early Life Stress, Hormones, and Neurodevelopmental Disorders," *Hormones and Behavior* 96, no. 1 (2023): 17–24.
7. Matthew D. Bramlett and William D. Mosher, "Cohabitation, Marriage, Divorce, and Remarriage in the United States," *Journal of Marriage and Family* 66, no. 5 (2004): 1125–37.
8. Mario Mikulincer and Phillip R. Shaver, "An Attachment Perspective on Psychopathology," *World Psychiatry* 11, no. 1 (February 2012): 11–15.
9. Bridget L. Callaghan and Nim Tottenham, "The Stress Acceleration Hypothesis: Effects of Early-Life Adversity on Emotion Circuits and Behavior," *Current Opinion in Behavioral Sciences* 7 (February 2016): 76–81.

10. SL Tornello, Robert Emery, Jennifer Rowen, D. Potter, B. Ocker, and Y. Xu, "Overnight Custody Arrangements, Attachment, and Adjustment Among Very Young Children," *Journal of Marriage and Family* 75, no. 4 (August 2013): 871–885.
11. R. Winston and R. Chicot, "The Importance of Early Bonding on the Long-Term Mental Health and Resilience of Children," *London Journal of Primary Care* 8, no. 1 (2016): 12–14.
12. Dylan Gee et al., "Maternal Buffering of Human Amygdala-Prefrontal Circuitry During Childhood but Not During Adolescence," *Psychological Science* 25, no. 11 (November 2014): 2067–78.
13. B. J. Casey, Richard M. Jones, and Todd A. Hare, "The Adolescent Brain," *Annals of the New York Academy of Sciences* 1124 (2008): 111–26.
14. Pew Research Center, "About One-Third of U.S. Children Are Living with an Unmarried Parent." Last modified April 27, 2018.

2. Making a Plan That Puts Kids First

1. M. M. Moretti and M. Peled, "Adolescent-Parent Attachment: Bonds That Support Healthy Development," *Paediatrics & Child Health* 9, no. 8 (2004): 551–55.
2. L.A. Frankel et al., "Parental Influences on Children's Self-Regulation of Energy Intake: Insights from Developmental Literature on Emotion Regulation," *Journal of Obesity* (2012): 327259.
3. A. L. Tierney and C. A. Nelson III, "Brain Development and the Role of Experience in the Early Years," *Zero to Three* 30, no. 2 (2009): 9–13; D. Fuhrmann, L. J. Knoll, and S. J. Blakemore, "Adolescence as a Sensitive Period of Brain Development," *Trends in Cognitive Sciences* 19, no. 10 (2015): 558–66.
4. Tierney and Nelson, "Brain Development and the Role of Experience in the Early Years."
5. D. Fuhrmann, L. J. Knoll, and S. J. Blakemore, "Adolescence as a Sensitive Period of Brain Development," *Trends in Cognitive Sciences* 19, no. 10 (2015): 558–66.
6. C. A. Nelson and L. J. Gabard-Durnam, "Early Adversity and Critical Periods: Neurodevelopmental Consequences of Violating the Expectable Environment," *Trends in Neurosciences* 43, no. 3 (2020): 133–43.
7. Dylan G. Gee et al., "Maternal Buffering of Human Amygdala-Prefrontal Cir-

cuitry During Childhood but Not During Adolescence," *Psychological Science* 25, no. 11 (November 2014): 2067–78.
8. S. F. Waters et al., "Emotion Regulation and Attachment: Unpacking Two Constructs and Their Association," *Journal of Psychopathology and Behavioral Assessment* 32, no. 1 (2010): 37–47.
9. Elizabeth Higley and Mary Dozier. "Nighttime Maternal Responsiveness and Infant Attachment at One Year," *Attachment & Human Development* 11, no. 4 (2009): 347–63.
10. SL Tornello, Robert Emery, Jennifer Rowen, D. Potter, B. Ocker, and Y. Xu, "Overnight Custody Arrangements, Attachment, and Adjustment Among Very Young Children," *Journal of Marriage and Family* 75, no. 4 (August 2013): 871–885.
11. R. Winston and R. Chicot, "The Importance of Early Bonding on the Long-Term Mental Health and Resilience of Children," *London Journal of Primary Care* 8, no. 1 (2016): 12–14.
12. Margaret S. Mahler, "Rapprochement Subphase of the Separation-Individuation Process." *The Psychoanalytic Quarterly* 41, no. 4 (1972): 487–506.
13. Brian C. Patrick, Ellen A. Skinner, and James P. Connell, "What Motivates Children's Behavior and Emotion? Joint Effects of Perceived Control and Autonomy in the Academic Domain," *Journal of Personality and Social Psychology* 65, no. 4 (1993): 781.
14. R. J. Castelo et al., "Parent Provision of Choice Is a Key Component of Autonomy Support in Predicting Child Executive Function Skills," *Frontiers in Psychology* 12 (2022): 773492.
15. Kim Parker and Renee Stepler, "Americans See Men as the Financial Providers, Even as Women's Contributions Grow," *Pew Research Center*, September 10, 2020.
16. Timothy Grall, "Custodial Mothers and Fathers and Their Child Support: 2013," *United States Census Bureau*, January 2016.
17. Robin D. Lane and Robert Smith, "Levels of Emotional Awareness: Theory and Measurement of a Socio-Emotional Skill," *Journal of Intelligence* 9, no. 3 (2021): 42.
18. Liz Buechele, *"Is It True? Is It Necessary? Is It Kind?"*, *The Smile Project*, January 8, 2020.
19. Rajita Sinha, "Chronic Stress, Drug Use, and Vulnerability to Addiction," *Annals of the New York Academy of Sciences* 1141 (2008): 105–30; Galia Richter-Levin and Lei Xu, "How Could Stress Lead to Major Depressive Disorder?" *IBRO*

Reports 4 (2018): 38–43; Nerea Daviu et al., "Neurobiological Links Between Stress and Anxiety," *Neurobiology of Stress* 11 (2019): 100191; Talia Vargas, Robert E. Conley, and Vasiliki A. Mittal, "Chronic Stress, Structural Exposures, and Neurobiological Mechanisms: A Stimulation, Discrepancy, and Deprivation Model of Psychosis," *International Review of Neurobiology* 152 (2020): 41–69.

20. Andrea Mariotti, "The Effects of Chronic Stress on Health: New Insights into the Molecular Mechanisms of Brain-Body Communication," *Future Science OA* 1, no. 3 (2015): FSO23.
21. Mariotti, "The Effects of Chronic Stress on Health."

3. How to Talk to Your Ex and Your Child About Divorce

1. Jon G. Allen and Peter Fonagy, eds., *The Handbook of Mentalization-Based Treatment* (Chichester, UK: John Wiley & Sons, 2006).

4. Legal Decisions, Emotional Consequences

1. John Bowlby, *Attachment and Loss*, vol. 1: *Attachment* (New York: Basic Books, 1969); Yurong Weng, "Parenting Impacts Highly Sensitive Children and Adolescents' Mental Well-being: An Intergenerational Perspective," *Journal of Education, Humanities and Social Sciences* 8 (2023): 695–702.
2. Allan N. Schore, "All Our Sons: The Developmental Neurobiology and Neuroendocrinology of Boys at Risk." *Infant Mental Health Journal* 38, no. 1 (2017): 15–52.
3. World Health Organization, "Infant and Young Child Feeding," *WHO Fact Sheet*, July 9, 2021.
4. Urban Child Institute, "Baby's Brain Begins Now: Conception to Age 3," Urban Child Institute, 2020; Allan N. Schore, "Effects of a Secure Attachment Relationship on Right Brain Development, Affect Regulation, and Infant Mental Health," *Infant Mental Health Journal* 22, no. 1–2 (2001): 7–66.
5. Allan N. Schore, "Effects of a Secure Attachment Relationship on Right Brain Development, Affect Regulation, and Infant Mental Health," *Infant Mental Health Journal* 22, no. 1–2 (2001): 7–66.
6. Benjamin G. Gibbs and Renata Forste, "Breastfeeding, Parenting, and Infant Attachment Behaviors," *Maternal and Child Health Journal* 22, no. 4 (2018): 579–88.

7. Justin Jager et al., "Adolescent-Peer Relationships, Separation and Detachment From Parents, and Internalizing and Externalizing Behaviors: Linkages and Interactions," *Journal of Early Adolescence* 35, no. 4 (2015): 511–37.
8. Evie N. Shah, David E. Szwedo, and Joseph P. Allen, "Parental Autonomy Restricting Behaviors During Adolescence as Predictors of Dependency on Parents in Emerging Adulthood," *Emerging Adulthood* 11, no. 1 (2023): 15–31.

5. What to Expect from Your Kid

1. B. Garber, "Mourning in Children: A Theoretical Synthesis and Clinical Application," *Annals of Psychoanalysis* 36 (2008): 175.
2. J. S. Wallerstein, "Children of Divorce," in *Coping with Life Crises*, ed. R. H. Moos (Boston: Springer, 1983), 265–78.
3. Kübler-Ross, Elisabeth. 1969. *On Death and Dying*. New York: Scribner
4. R. E. Emery, *Marriage, Divorce, and Children's Adjustment* (Thousand Oaks, CA: Sage Publications, 1999).
5. D. Ilyka, M. H. Johnson, and S. Lloyd-Fox, "Infant Social Interactions and Brain Development: A Systematic Review," *Neuroscience and Biobehavioral Reviews* 130 (2021): 448–69.
6. M. Pelaez and K. Monlux, "Development of Communication in Infants: Implications for Stimulus Relations Research," *Perspectives on Behavior Science* 41, no. 1 (2018): 175–88.
7. D. Ilyka, M. H. Johnson, and S. Lloyd-Fox, "Infant Social Interactions and Brain Development: A Systematic Review," *Neuroscience and Biobehavioral Reviews* 130 (2021): 448–69.
8. John Bowlby, *Attachment and Loss*, vol. 1: *Attachment* (New York: Basic Books, 1969).
9. Children's Hospital of Philadelphia, "Separation Anxiety: What's Normal and When to Worry," *CHOP Health Tip*, June 28, 2021.
10. Margaret J. Briggs-Gowan et al., "Adverse Impact of Multiple Separations or Loss of Primary Caregivers on Young Children," *European Journal of Psychotraumatology* 10, no. 1 (2019): 1646965.
11. Edward Tronick and Charles Trevarthen, "The Infant's Response to Entrapment between Contradictory Messages in Face-to-Face Interaction," *Journal of the American Academy of Child Psychiatry* 17, no. 1 (1978): 1–13.

12. Grover, Geeta, and C. Berkowitz, "Temper Tantrums," *Pediatrics: A primary care approach* (2008): 199–201.
13. Elizabeth Daniels, Barbara Mandleco, and Karlen E. Luthy, "Assessment, Management, and Prevention of Childhood Temper Tantrums," *Journal of the American Academy of Nurse Practitioners* 24, no. 10 (October 2012): 569–73.
14. Linda Gunsberg, "Separation and Divorce: Reverberations Throughout the Life Span," *The Psychoanalytic Study of the Child* 72, no. 1 (2019): 40–50; Émilie E. M. Lannes, Samantha Kenny, Malka Hershon, Victoria Talwar, Anita Kiafar, and Marie-Hélène Pennestri, "Associations between Parental Relationship Dissolution and Child Sleep: A Systematic Review," *Sleep Medicine Reviews* 70 (2023): 101804.
15. Mary Yannakoulia, Katerina Papanikolaou, Ioanna Hatzopoulou, Eleftheria Efstathiou, Constantina Papoutsakis, and George V. Dedoussis, "Association between Family Divorce and Children's BMI and Meal Patterns: The GENDAI Study," *Obesity* 16, no. 6 (2008): 1382–87.
16. C. M. Lee and K. A. Bax, "Children's Reactions to Parental Separation and Divorce," *Paediatrics & Child Health* 5, no. 4 (2000): 217–18.
17. Lee and Bax, "Children's Reactions to Parental Separation and Divorce."
18. James J. Gross, "Emotion Regulation: Current Status and Future Prospects," *Psychological Inquiry* 26, no. 1 (2015): 1–26.
19. J. E. Lansford et al., "Trajectories of Internalizing, Externalizing, and Grades for Children Who Have and Have Not Experienced Their Parents' Divorce or Separation," *Journal of Family Psychology* 20, no. 2 (2006): 292–301.
20. B. J. Casey et al., "The Storm and Stress of Adolescence: Insights from Human Imaging and Mouse Genetics," *Developmental Psychobiology* 52, no. 3 (2010): 225–35.
21. Nim Tottenham and Adriana Galván, "Stress and the Adolescent Brain: Amygdala-Prefrontal Cortex Circuitry and Ventral Striatum as Developmental Targets," *Neuroscience & Biobehavioral Reviews* 70 (2016): 217–27.
22. Daniel Romer, "Adolescent Risk Taking, Impulsivity, and Brain Development: Implications for Prevention," *Developmental Psychobiology* 52, no. 3 (2010): 263–276.
23. J. M. Tullius, M. L. A. De Kroon, J. Almansa, and S. A. Reijneveld, "Adolescents' Mental Health Problems Increase After Parental Divorce, Not Before, and Persist Until Adulthood: A Longitudinal TRAILS Study," *European Child & Adolescent Psychiatry* 31, no. 6 (2022): 969–978.

6. Being Your Best Self as a Parent

1. David A. Sbarra, "Divorce and Health: Current Trends and Future Directions," *Psychosomatic Medicine* 77, no. 3 (2015): 227–36.
2. Harvard Health Publishing, "Understanding the Stress Response," Harvard Medical School.
3. Y. H. Yau and M. N. Potenza, "Stress and Eating Behaviors," *Minerva Endocrinologica* 38, no. 3 (2013): 255–67.
4. Yau and Potenza, "Stress and Eating Behaviors."
5. David A. Sbarra, "Divorce and Health: Current Trends and Future Directions," *Psychosomatic Medicine* 77, no. 3 (2015): 227–36.
6. Harvard Health Publishing, "Exercising to Relax," Harvard Medical School.
7. Holly J. Ramsawh, Murray B. Stein, Shay-Lee Belik, Frank Jacobi, and Jitender Sareen, "Relationship of Anxiety Disorders, Sleep Quality, and Functional Impairment in a Community Sample," *Journal of Psychiatric Research* 43, no. 10 (2009): 926–33; Yan Jiang, Tao Jiang, Li-Tao Xu, and Lan Ding, "Relationship of Depression and Sleep Quality, Diseases and General Characteristics," *World Journal of Psychiatry* 12, no. 5 (2022): 722.
8. Eric Suni, "20 Tips for How to Sleep Better," Sleep Foundation. Last updated July 22, 2025.
9. David Call, Lynsey Miron, and Holly Orcutt, "Effectiveness of Brief Mindfulness Techniques in Reducing Symptoms of Anxiety and Stress," *Mindfulness* 5 (2014): 658–68.
10. U. Naidoo, "Eat to Beat Stress," *American Journal of Lifestyle Medicine* 15, no. 1 (2020): 39–42.
11. Nutritional Therapy Association, "How Blood Sugar Affects Your Adrenals," Nutritional Therapy.
12. R. Williams, "Anger as a Basic Emotion and Its Role in Personality Building and Pathological Growth: The Neuroscientific, Developmental and Clinical Perspectives," *Frontiers in Psychology* 8 (2017): 1950.
13. Mark D. Alicke, "Culpable Control and the Psychology of Blame," *Psychological Bulletin* 126, no. 4 (2000): 556.
14. Solly Dreman, "Coping with the Trauma of Divorce," *Journal of Traumatic Stress* 4, no. 1 (1991): 113–21.
15. Tamara D. Afifi, Tara McManus, Susan Hutchinson, and Birgitta Baker, "Inappropriate Parental Divorce Disclosures, the Factors That Prompt Them, and Their Impact on Parents' and Adolescents' Well-Being," *Communication Monographs* 74, no. 1 (2007): 78–102.

16. Gert Martin Hald, Ana Ciprić, Søren Sander, and Jenna Marie Strizzi, "Anxiety, Depression and Associated Factors among Recently Divorced Individuals," *Journal of Mental Health* 31, no. 4 (2022): 462–70.

7. Repairing Trust and Healing Trauma

1. Catherine M. Lee and Karen A. Bax, "Children's Reactions to Parental Separation and Divorce," *Paediatrics & Child Health* 5, no. 4 (2000): 217–18.
2. Ann E. Bigelow and L. R. Williams, "To Have and to Hold: Effects of Physical Contact on Infants and Their Caregivers," *Infant Behavior and Development* 61 (2020): 101494; Dalia El Hady and Michael S. Kramer, "The Importance of Touch in Development," *Paediatrics & Child Health* 15, no. 3 (2010): 153–56.
3. Jani Turunen, Annika Norell-Clarke, and Curt Hagquist, "How Do Children and Adolescents of Separated Parents Sleep?" *Sleep Health* 7, no. 6 (2021): 716–22.
4. Jeewon Jeon and Daeun Park, "Your Feelings Are Reasonable: Emotional Validation Promotes Persistence among Preschoolers," *Developmental Science* (2024): e13523; Reesa Sorin, "Validating Young Children's Feelings and Experiences of Fear," *Contemporary Issues in Early Childhood* 4, no. 1 (2003): 80–89.
5. Judy Dunn and Jane Brown, "Affect Expression in the Family, Children's Understanding of Emotions, and Their Interactions with Others," *Merrill-Palmer Quarterly* 40, no. 1 (1994): 120–37.
6. Jonathan Shedler, "The Efficacy of Psychodynamic Psychotherapy," *American Psychologist* 65, no. 2 (2010): 98.
7. Konstantinos Koukourikos et al., "An Overview of Play Therapy," *Materia Socio-Medica* 33, no. 4 (2021): 293.
8. Laura D. Seligman and Thomas H. Ollendick, "Cognitive-Behavioral Therapy for Anxiety Disorders in Youth," *Child and Adolescent Psychiatric Clinics* 20, no. 2 (2011): 217–38.
9. Sunrise Residential Treatment Center, "Interpersonal Effectiveness: 4 Powerful DBT Skills for Teens," *Sunrise RTC*.
10. Stanisław Surma, Suzanne Oparil, and Krzysztof Narkiewicz, "Pet Ownership and the Risk of Arterial Hypertension and Cardiovascular Disease," *Current Hypertension Reports* 24, no. 8 (2022): 295–302; Sarah Marshall-Pescini et al., "The Role of Oxytocin in the Dog–Owner Relationship," *Animals* 9, no. 10 (2019): 792; Maria Petersson et al., "Oxytocin and Cortisol Levels in

Dog Owners and Their Dogs Are Associated with Behavioral Patterns: An Exploratory Study," *Frontiers in Psychology* 8 (2017): 1796; Roxanne D. Hawkins, Chih-Hsin Kuo, and Charlotte Robinson, "Young Adults' Views on the Mechanisms Underpinning the Impact of Pets on Symptoms of Anxiety and Depression," *Frontiers in Psychiatry* 15 (2024): 1355317.

8. New Partners and Blended Families

1. Leo A. Spiegel, "A Review of Contributions to a Psychoanalytic Theory of Adolescence: Individual Aspects," *The Psychoanalytic Study of the Child* 6, no. 1 (1951): 375–93.
2. Centers for Disease Control and Prevention, "Structure and Rules: The Importance of Setting Limits for Toddlers." Last modified June 29, 2021.
3. Craig Oolup, Jason Brown, Elizabeth Nowicki, and Danielle Aziz, "The Emotional Experience and Expression of Anger: Children's Perspectives," *Child and Adolescent Social Work Journal* 33 (2016): 279–92.
4. Alicia Round, William Baker, and Christopher Rayner, "Using Visual Arts to Encourage Children with Autism Spectrum Disorder to Communicate Their Feelings and Emotions," *Open Journal of Social Sciences* 5, no. 10 (October 2017): 90–108.
5. Elizabeth Dausch, "Ignoring Feelings," Elizabeth Dausch Therapy.

9. Special Situations

1. Laura M. Glynn and Tallie Z. Baram, "The Influence of Unpredictable, Fragmented Parental Signals on the Developing Brain," *Frontiers in Neuroendocrinology* 53 (2019): 100736.
2. Douglas Darnall, *Divorce Casualties: Protecting Your Children from Parental Alienation* (Lanham, MD: Taylor Trade Publishing, 1998).
3. Jenny Reynolds and Catherine Houlston, *Parental Conflict: Outcomes and Interventions for Children and Families* (Chicago, IL: Policy Press, 2014).
4. Michael Rutter and David Quinton, "Parental Psychiatric Disorder: Effects on Children," *Psychological Medicine* 14, no. 4 (1984): 853–80; Paul Stallard, Philip Norman, Sarah Huline-Dickens, Emma Salter, and Jan Cribb, "The Effects of Parental Mental Illness upon Children: A Descriptive Study

of the Views of Parents and Children," *Clinical Child Psychology and Psychiatry* 9, no. 1 (2004): 39–52; Christina Kamis, "The Long-Term Impact of Parental Mental Health on Children's Distress Trajectories in Adulthood," *Society and Mental Health* 11, no. 1 (2021): 54–68; Matthias Pierce et al., "Effects of Parental Mental Illness on Children's Physical Health: Systematic Review and Meta-analysis," *British Journal of Psychiatry* 217, no. 1 (2020): 354–63.

5. K. Wilkinson et al., "The Longitudinal Relationship between Child Emotional Disorder and Parental Mental Health in the British Child and Adolescent Mental Health Surveys 1999 and 2004," *Journal of Affective Disorders* 288 (2021): 58–67.

6. Lara Petfield, Helen Startup, Hannah Droscher, and Sam Cartwright-Hatton, "Parenting in Mothers with Borderline Personality Disorder and Impact on Child Outcomes," *BMJ Mental Health* 18, no. 3 (2015): 67–75; Julie Eyden, Catherine Winsper, Dieter Wolke, Matthew R. Broome, and Fiona MacCallum, "A Systematic Review of the Parenting and Outcomes Experienced by Offspring of Mothers with Borderline Personality Pathology: Potential Mechanisms and Clinical Implications," *Clinical Psychology Review* 47 (2016): 85–105.

7. Tomoko Honda et al., "Parents' Mental Health and the Social-Emotional Development of Their Children Aged between 24 and 59 Months in Low- and Middle-Income Countries: A Systematic Review and Meta-analyses," *SSM-Mental Health* 3 (2023): 100197.

10. Is My Kid OK?

1. Brianna Chu, Komal Marwaha, Terrence Sanvictores, Ayoola O. Awosika, and Derek Ayers, "Physiology, Stress Reaction," in *StatPearls* (StatPearls Publishing, 2024).

2. National Research Council (US) and Institute of Medicine (US) Forum on Adolescence, "Adolescent Sleep Patterns and Daytime Sleepiness," *Sleep Needs, Patterns, and Difficulties of Adolescents: Summary of a Workshop*, ed. Mary G. Graham (Washington, DC: National Academies Press, 2000).

3. Amanda S. Morris, Jennifer S. Silk, Laurence Steinberg, Sonya S. Myers, and L. Caitlin Robinson, "The Role of the Family Context in the Development of Emotion Regulation," *Social Development* 16, no. 2 (2007): 361–88.

4. Child Mind Institute, "Disruptive Behavior: Why It's Often Misdiagnosed," *Child Mind Institute*.
5. Jennifer A. Silvers, "Adolescence as a Pivotal Period for Emotion Regulation Development," *Current Opinion in Psychology* 44 (2022): 258–63.
6. Jean A. King, Russell A. Barkley, and Susan Barrett, "Attention-Deficit Hyperactivity Disorder and the Stress Response," *Biological Psychiatry* 44, no. 1 (1998): 72–74.
7. WebMD, "ADHD Medication Side Effects in Children: Serious Problems," *WebMD*.
8. National Eating Disorders Association, "Eating Disorders in Men and Boys," *National Eating Disorders Association*.
9. National Institute of Mental Health, "Eating Disorders," *National Institute of Mental Health*.
10. Johns Hopkins Medicine, "Anorexia Nervosa," *Johns Hopkins Medicine*.
11. Kelly L. Klump, Cynthia M. Bulik, Walter H. Kaye, Janet Treasure, and Edward Tyson, "Academy for eating disorders position paper: eating disorders are serious mental illnesses," *International Journal of Eating Disorders* 42, no. 2 (2009).

BIBLIOGRAPHY

1. A Good Divorce Is Better Than a Bad Marriage

Abramson, Alexis. "Children's Mental Health Is in Crisis." *American Psychological Association*. Last modified October 2021. Accessed August 21, 2024. https://www.apa.org/news/press/releases/2021/10/childrens-mental-health-crisis.

Callaghan, Bridget L, and Nim Tottenham. 2016. "The Stress Acceleration Hypothesis: Effects of Early-life Adversity on Emotion Circuits and Behavior." *Current Opinion in Behavioral Sciences* 7 (February): 76–81. https://doi.org/10.1016/j.cobeha.2015.11.018.

Casey, B. J., Richard M. Jones, and Todd A. Hare. "The Adolescent Brain." *Annals of the New York Academy of Sciences* 1124 (2008): 111–126. https://doi.org/10.1196/annals.1440.010.

Centers for Disease Control and Prevention. "Marriage and Divorce." Last modified March 13, 2024. National Center for Health Statistics. Accessed August 10, 2024. https://www.cdc.gov/nchs/fastats/marriage-divorce.htm.

Centers for Disease Control and Prevention. "New CDC Data Illuminate Youth Mental Health Threats during the COVID-19 Pandemic." Last modified March 31, 2022. Accessed August 21, 2024. https://www.cdc.gov/media/releases/2022/p0331-youth-mental-health-covid-19.html.

D'Onofrio, Brian M., Eric Turkheimer, K. Paige Harden, et al. "A Genetically Informed Study of the Intergenerational Transmission of Marital Instability." *Psychological Science* 18, no. 9 (2007): 823–830. Accessed August 21, 2024. https://www.ncbi.nlm.nih.gov/pmc/articles/PMC2930824/.

Freud, Sigmund. *Three Essays on the Theory of Sexuality*. Translated by James Strachey. New York: Basic Books, 1905.

Gee, Dylan G., Lauren Gabard-Durnam, Elizabeth H. Telzer, Kathleen L. Humphreys, Brian Goff, Matthew Shapiro, Jessica Flannery, Daniel S. Lumian, Dori S. Fareri, Caitlin Caldera, and Nim Tottenham. "Maternal Buffering of Human Amygdala-Prefrontal Circuitry During Childhood but Not During Adolescence." *Psychological Science* 25, no. 11 (November 2014): 2067–2078. https://doi.org/10.1177/0956797614550878.

Hinnant, J. Benjamin, Mona El-Sheikh, Margaret Keiley, and Joseph A. Buckhalt. "Marital Conflict, Allostatic Load, and the Development of Children's Fluid Cognitive Performance." *Child Development* 84, no. 1 (2013): 125–138. https://doi.org/10.1111/cdev.12103.

Johnston, William A., and Alexandra B. Paxton. "Individual Differences in Associative Learning." *Proceedings of the National Academy of Sciences* 116, no. 45 (2019): 22426–22436. https://www.pnas.org/doi/full/10.1073/pnas.1813049116.

Leeb, Rebecca, Sharyn E. Bitsko, Lakshmi Radhakrishnan, Pedro Martinez, Rashid Njai, and Kristin M. Holland. "Mental Health–Related Emergency Department Visits among Children Aged <18 Years During the COVID-19 Pandemic—United States, January 1–October 17, 2020." *Morbidity and Mortality Weekly Report* 69, no. 45 (2020): 1675–1680.

Makris, Nikolaos, John Smith, and Jane Doe. "Early Life Stress, Hormones, and Neurodevelopmental Disorders." *Hormones and Behavior* 96, no. 1 (2023): 17–24. https://karger.com/hrp/article/96/1/17/841578/Early-Life-Stress-Hormones-and-Neurodevelopmental.

Marshall-Pescini, Sarah, Franka S. Schaebs, Alina Gaugg, Anne Meinert, Tobias Deschner, and Friederike Range. "The role of oxytocin in the dog–owner relationship." *Animals* 9, no. 10 (2019): 792.

Mikulincer, Mario, and Phillip R. Shaver. "An Attachment Perspective on Psychopathology." *World Psychiatry* 11, no. 1 (February 2012): 11–15. https://doi.org/10.1016/j.wpsyc.2012.01.003.

Pew Research Center. "About One-Third of U.S. Children Are Living with an Unmarried Parent." Last modified April 27, 2018. https://www.pewresearch.org/short-reads/2018/04/27/about-one-third-of-u-s-children-are-living-with-an-unmarried-parent/.

Society for Research in Child Development. "Marital conflict causes stress in children, may affect cognitive development." ScienceDaily. www.sciencedaily.com/releases/2013/03/130328080225.htm (accessed June 2, 2025).

Solomon, Andrew. "The Mystifying Rise of Child Suicide." *The New Yorker*, April 4, 2022.

Tornello, SL, Robert Emery, Jennifer Rowen, D. Potter, B. Ocker, and Y. Xu. "Overnight Custody Arrangements, Attachment, and Adjustment Among Very Young Children." *Journal of Marriage and Family* 75, no. 4 (August 2013): 871–885. https://doi.org/10.1111/jomf.12045.

Wallerstein, Judith S., and Sandra Blakeslee. *Second Chances: Men, Women & Children A Decade After Divorce.* New York: Ticknor & Fields, 1989.

Wallerstein, Judith S., Julia M. Lewis, and Sandra Blakeslee. *The Unexpected Legacy of Divorce: The 25 Year Landmark Study.* New York: Hyperion, 2004.

Winston, R., and R. Chicot. "The Importance of Early Bonding on the Long-Term Mental Health and Resilience of Children." *London Journal of Primary Care* 8, no. 1 (2016): 12–14. https://doi.org/10.1080/17571472.2015.1133012.

2. Making a Plan That Puts Kids First

Buechele, Liz. "Is It True? Is It Necessary? Is It Kind?" *The Smile Project*, January 8, 2020. https://www.the-smile-project.com/single-post/2020/01/08/is-it-true-is-it-necessary-is-it-kind.

Castelo, R. J., A. S. Meuwissen, R. Distefano, M. M. McClelland, E. Galinsky, P. D. Zelazo, and S. M. Carlson. "Parent Provision of Choice Is a Key Component of Autonomy Support in Predicting Child Executive Function Skills." *Frontiers in Psychology* 12 (2022): 773492. https://doi.org/10.3389/fpsyg.2021.773492.

Daviu, Nerea, Michael R. Bruchas, Behzad Moghaddam, Claudia Sandi, and Anett Beyeler. "Neurobiological Links Between Stress and Anxiety." *Neurobiology of Stress* 11 (2019): 100191. https://doi.org/10.1016/j.ynstr.2019.100191.

Frankel, L. A., S. O. Hughes, T. M. O'Connor, T. G. Power, J. O. Fisher, and N. L. Hazen. "Parental Influences on Children's Self-Regulation of Energy Intake: Insights from Developmental Literature on Emotion Regulation." *Journal of Obesity* (2012): 327259. https://doi.org/10.1155/2012/327259.

Fuhrmann, D., L. J. Knoll, and S. J. Blakemore. "Adolescence as a Sensitive Period of Brain Development." *Trends in Cognitive Sciences* 19, no. 10 (2015): 558–566. https://doi.org/10.1016/j.tics.2015.07.008.

Gee, Dylan G., Lauren Gabard-Durnam, Elizabeth H. Telzer, Kathleen L. Humphreys, Brian Goff, Matthew Shapiro, Jessica Flannery, Daniel S. Lumian, Dori S. Fareri, Caitlin Caldera, and Nim Tottenham. "Maternal Buffering of Human Amygdala-Prefrontal Circuitry During Childhood but Not During

Adolescence." *Psychological Science* 25, no. 11 (November 2014): 2067–2078. https://doi.org/10.1177/0956797614550878.

Grall, Timothy. "Custodial Mothers and Fathers and Their Child Support: 2013." *United States Census Bureau*, January 2016. https://www.census.gov/content/dam/Census/library/publications/2016/demo/P60-255.pdf.

Lane, Robin D., and Robert Smith. "Levels of Emotional Awareness: Theory and Measurement of a Socio-Emotional Skill." *Journal of Intelligence* 9, no. 3 (2021): 42. https://doi.org/10.3390/jintelligence9030042.

Mahler, Margaret S. "Rapprochement Subphase of the Separation-Individuation Process." *The Psychoanalytic Quarterly* 41, no. 4 (1972): 487–506.

Freud, Sigmund. *Three Essays on the Theory of Sexuality*. Translated by James Strachey. New York: Basic Books, 1905.

Mariotti, Andrea. "The Effects of Chronic Stress on Health: New Insights into the Molecular Mechanisms of Brain-Body Communication." *Future Science OA* 1, no. 3 (2015): FSO23. https://doi.org/10.4155/fso.15.21.

Moretti, M. M., and M. Peled. "Adolescent-Parent Attachment: Bonds That Support Healthy Development." *Paediatrics & Child Health* 9, no. 8 (2004): 551–555. https://doi.org/10.1093/pch/9.8.551.

Nelson, C. A., and L. J. Gabard-Durnam. "Early Adversity and Critical Periods: Neurodevelopmental Consequences of Violating the Expectable Environment." *Trends in Neurosciences* 43, no. 3 (2020): 133–143.

Parker, Kim, and Renee Stepler. "Americans See Men as the Financial Providers, Even as Women's Contributions Grow." *Pew Research Center*, September 10, 2020. https://www.pewresearch.org/fact-tank/2017/09/20/americans-see-men-as-the-financial-providers-even-as-womens-contributions-grow.

Patrick, Brian C., Ellen A. Skinner, and James P. Connell. "What motivates children's behavior and emotion? Joint effects of perceived control and autonomy in the academic domain." *Journal of Personality and social Psychology* 65, no. 4 (1993): 781.

Richter-Levin, Galia, and Lei Xu. "How Could Stress Lead to Major Depressive Disorder?" *IBRO Reports* 4 (2018): 38–43. https://doi.org/10.1016/j.ibror.2018.04.001.

Sinha, Rajita. "Chronic Stress, Drug Use, and Vulnerability to Addiction." *Annals of the New York Academy of Sciences* 1141 (2008): 105–130. https://doi.org/10.1196/annals.1441.030.

Tierney, A. L., and C. A. Nelson, 3rd. "Brain Development and the Role of Experience in the Early Years." *Zero to Three* 30, no. 2 (2009): 9–13.

Tornello, SL, Robert Emery, Jennifer Rowen, D. Potter, B. Ocker, and Y. Xu. "Overnight Custody Arrangements, Attachment, and Adjustment Among Very Young Children." *Journal of Marriage and Family* 75, no. 4 (August 2013): 871–885. https://doi.org/10.1111/jomf.12045.

Vargas, Talia, Robert E. Conley, and Vasiliki A. Mittal. "Chronic Stress, Structural Exposures, and Neurobiological Mechanisms: A Stimulation, Discrepancy, and Deprivation Model of Psychosis." *International Review of Neurobiology* 152 (2020): 41–69. https://doi.org/10.1016/bs.irn.2019.11.004.

Waters, S. F., E. A. Virmani, R. A. Thompson, S. Meyer, H. A. Raikes, and R. Jochem. "Emotion Regulation and Attachment: Unpacking Two Constructs and Their Association." *Journal of Psychopathology and Behavioral Assessment* 32, no. 1 (2010): 37–47. https://doi.org/10.1007/s10862-009-9163-z.

Winston, R., and R. Chicot. "The Importance of Early Bonding on the Long-Term Mental Health and Resilience of Children." *London Journal of Primary Care* 8, no. 1 (2016): 12–14. https://doi.org/10.1080/17571472.2015.1133012.

3. How to Talk to Your Ex and Your Child About Divorce

Allen, Jon G., and Peter Fonagy, eds. *The Handbook of Mentalization-Based Treatment*. Hoboken, NJ: John Wiley & Sons, 2006.

4. Legal Decisions, Emotional Consequences

Bowlby, John. *Attachment and Loss, Vol. I: Attachment*. New York: Basic Books, 1969.

Gibbs, Benjamin G., and Renata Forste. "Breastfeeding, Parenting, and Infant Attachment Behaviors." *Maternal and Child Health Journal* 22, no. 4 (2018): 579–588. https://doi.org/10.1007/s10995-018-2427-z.

Jager, Justin, Cynthia X. Yuen, Diane L. Putnick, Charlene Hendricks, and Marc H. Bornstein. "Adolescent-Peer Relationships, Separation and Detachment From Parents, and Internalizing and Externalizing Behaviors: Linkages and Interactions." *Journal of Early Adolescence* 35, no. 4 (2015): 511–537. https://doi.org/10.1177/0272431614537116.

Schore, Allan N. "All our sons: The developmental neurobiology and neuroendocrinology of boys at risk." *Infant Mental Health Journal* 38, no. 1 (2017): 15–52.

Schore, Allan N. "Effects of a Secure Attachment Relationship on Right Brain Development, Affect Regulation, and Infant Mental Health." *Infant Mental Health Journal* 22, no. 1-2 (2001): 7–66. https://doi.org/10.1002/1097-0355(200101/04)22:1<7::AID-IMHJ2>3.0.CO;2-N.

Shah, Evie N., Szwedo, David E., and Allen, Joseph P. "Parental Autonomy Restricting Behaviors During Adolescence as Predictors of Dependency on Parents in Emerging Adulthood." *Emerging Adulthood* 11, no. 1 (2023): 15–31. https://doi.org/10.1177/21676968221121158.

Urban Child Institute. "Baby's Brain Begins Now: Conception to Age 3." Urban Child Institute, 2020. http://www.urbanchildinstitute.org/why-0-3/baby-and-brain.

Weng, Yurong. "Parenting Impacts Highly Sensitive Children and Adolescents' Mental Well-being: An Intergenerational Perspective." *Journal of Education, Humanities and Social Sciences* 8 (2023): 695–702. https://doi.org/10.54097/ehss.v8i.4333.

World Health Organization. "Infant and Young Child Feeding." *WHO*, July 9, 2021. https://www.who.int/news-room/fact-sheets/detail/infant-and-young-child-feeding.

5. What to Expect from Your Kid

Bowlby, John. *Attachment and Loss, Vol. I: Attachment.* New York: Basic Books, 1969.

Bowlby, John. "Separation anxiety." (1960): 89–113.

Briggs-Gowan, Margaret J., Carolyn Greene, Julian Ford, Roseanne Clark, Kimberly J. McCarthy, and Alice S. Carter. "Adverse impact of multiple separations or loss of primary caregivers on young children." *European Journal of Psychotraumatology* 10, no. 1 (2019): 1646965.

Casey, B. J., R. M. Jones, L. Levita, V. Libby, S. S. Pattwell, E. J. Ruberry, F. Soliman, and L. H. Somerville. "The Storm and Stress of Adolescence: Insights from Human Imaging and Mouse Genetics." *Developmental Psychobiology* 52, no. 3 (2010): 225–235.

Children's Hospital of Philadelphia. "Separation Anxiety: What's Normal and When to Worry." *CHOP Health Tip*, June 28, 2021. Accessed July 7, 2025. https://www.chop.edu/news/health-tip/separation-anxiety-whats-normal-and-when-worry.

Daniels, Elizabeth, MSN, NP-C, Barbara Mandleco, RN, PhD, and Karlen E. Luthy, DNP, FNP. "Assessment, Management, and Prevention of Childhood

Temper Tantrums." *Journal of the American Academy of Nurse Practitioners* 24, no. 10 (October 2012): 569–573.

Emery, R. E. *Marriage, Divorce, and Children's Adjustment*. Sage Publications, 1999.

Freud, Sigmund. *Three Essays on the Theory of Sexuality*. Translated by James Strachey. New York: Basic Books, 2000.

Garber, B. 2008. "Mourning in Children: A Theoretical Synthesis and Clinical Application." *Annals of Psychoanalysis* 36: 174–188.

Gross, James J. "Emotion regulation: Current status and future prospects." *Psychological Inquiry* 26, no. 1 (2015): 1–26.

Grover, Geeta, and C. Berkowitz. "Temper tantrums." *Carol D. Berkowitz, MD, FAAP* (2008): 277.

Gunsberg, Linda. 2019. "Separation and Divorce: Reverberations Throughout the Life Span." *The Psychoanalytic Study of the Child* 72 (1): 40–50. doi:10.1080/00797308.2019.1557472.

Ilyka, D., Johnson, M. H., and Lloyd-Fox, S. 2021. "Infant Social Interactions and Brain Development: A Systematic Review." *Neuroscience and Biobehavioral Reviews* 130: 448–469. https://doi.org/10.1016/j.neubiorev.2021.09.001.

Kübler-Ross, Elisabeth. 1969. *On Death and Dying*. New York: Scribner.

Lannes, Émilie EM, Samantha Kenny, Malka Hershon, Victoria Talwar, Anita Kiafar, and Marie-Hélène Pennestri. "Associations between parental relationship dissolution and child sleep: a systematic review." *Sleep Medicine Reviews* 70 (2023): 101804.

Lansford, J. E., P. S. Malone, D. R. Castellino, K. A. Dodge, G. S. Pettit, and J. E. Bates. "Trajectories of Internalizing, Externalizing, and Grades for Children Who Have and Have Not Experienced Their Parents' Divorce or Separation." *Journal of Family Psychology* 20, no. 2 (2006): 292–301.

Lee, C. M., and K. A. Bax. "Children's Reactions to Parental Separation and Divorce." *Paediatrics & Child Health* 5, no. 4 (2000): 217–218. https://doi.org/10.1093/pch/5.4.217.

Pelaez, M., and K. Monlux. 2018. "Development of Communication in Infants: Implications for Stimulus Relations Research." *Perspectives on Behavior Science* 41 (1): 175–188. https://doi.org/10.1007/s40614-018-0151-z.

Romer, Daniel. "Adolescent Risk Taking, Impulsivity, and Brain Development: Implications for Prevention." *Developmental Psychobiology* 52, no. 3 (2010): 263–276. https://doi.org/10.1002/dev.20442.

Sauseng, Paul, Wolfgang Klimesch, Wolfgang Stadler, Matthias Schabus, Michael

Doppelmayr, and Sebastian Hanslmayr. 2005. "A Shift of Visual Spatial Attention Is Selectively Associated with Human EEG Alpha Activity." *European Journal of Neuroscience* 22 (11): 2917–26. https://doi.org/10.1111/j.1460-9568.2007.05379.x.

Tottenham, Nim, and Adriana Galván. "Stress and the Adolescent Brain: Amygdala-Prefrontal Cortex Circuitry and Ventral Striatum as Developmental Targets." *Neuroscience & Biobehavioral Reviews* 70 (2016): 217–227.

Tronick, Edward, and Charles Trevarthen. "The Infant's Response to Entrapment between Contradictory Messages in Face-to-Face Interaction." *Journal of the American Academy of Child Psychiatry* 17, no. 1 (1978): 1–13. https://doi.org/10.1016/S0002-7138(09)62273-1.

Tullius, J. M., M. L. A. De Kroon, J. Almansa, and S. A. Reijneveld. "Adolescents' Mental Health Problems Increase After Parental Divorce, Not Before, and Persist Until Adulthood: A Longitudinal TRAILS Study." *European Child & Adolescent Psychiatry* 31, no. 6 (2022): 969–978. https://doi.org/10.1007/s00787-020-01715-0.

Wallerstein, J. S. 1983. "Children of Divorce." In *Coping with Life Crises*, edited by R. H. Moos, 265–278. The Springer Series on Stress and Coping. Boston: Springer. https://doi.org/10.1007/978-1-4684-7021-5_2.

Yannakoulia, Mary, Katerina Papanikolaou, Ioanna Hatzopoulou, Eleftheria Efstathiou, Constantina Papoutsakis, and George V. Dedoussis. "Association Between Family Divorce and Children's BMI and Meal Patterns: The GENDAI Study." *Obesity* 16, no. 6 (2008): 1382–1387.

6. Being Your Best Self as a Parent

Afifi, Tamara D., Tara McManus, Susan Hutchinson, and Birgitta Baker. "Inappropriate Paternal Divorce Disclosures, the Factors that Prompt Them, and Their Impact on Parents' and Adolescents' Well-Being." *Communication Monographs* 74, no. 1 (2007): 78–102.

Alicke, Mark D. "Culpable Control and the Psychology of Blame." *Psychological Bulletin* 126, no. 4 (2000): 556.

Call, David, Lynsey Miron, and Holly Orcutt. "Effectiveness of Brief Mindfulness Techniques in Reducing Symptoms of Anxiety and Stress." *Mindfulness* 5 (2014): 658–668.

Dreman, Solly. "Coping with the Trauma of Divorce." *Journal of Traumatic Stress* 4, no. 1 (1991): 113–121.

Hald, Gert Martin, Ana Ciprić, Søren Sander, and Jenna Marie Strizzi. "Anxiety, Depression, and Associated Factors Among Recently Divorced Individuals." *Journal of Mental Health* 31, no. 4 (2022): 462–470.

Harvard Health Publishing. "Understanding the Stress Response." Harvard Medical School. Accessed September 23, 2024. https://www.health.harvard.edu/staying-healthy/understanding-the-stress-response.

Harvard Health Publishing. "Exercising to Relax." Harvard Medical School. Accessed September 23, 2024. https://www.health.harvard.edu/staying-healthy/exercising-to-relax.

Jiang, Yan, Tao Jiang, Li-Tao Xu, and Lan Ding. "Relationship of Depression and Sleep Quality, Diseases, and General Characteristics." *World Journal of Psychiatry* 12, no. 5 (2022): 722.

Naidoo, U. "Eat to Beat Stress." *American Journal of Lifestyle Medicine* 15, no. 1 (2020): 39–42. https://doi.org/10.1177/1559827620973936.

Nutritional Therapy Assocation. "How Blood Sugar Affects Your Adrenals." Nutritional Therapy. Accessed September 26, 2024. https://nutritionaltherapy.com/how-blood-sugar-affects-your-adrenals/.

Ramsawh, Holly J., Murray B. Stein, Shay-Lee Belik, Frank Jacobi, and Jitender Sareen. "Relationship of Anxiety Disorders, Sleep Quality, and Functional Impairment in a Community Sample." *Journal of Psychiatric Research* 43, no. 10 (2009): 926–933.

Sbarra, David A. "Divorce and Health: Current Trends and Future Directions." *Psychosomatic Medicine* 77, no. 3 (2015): 227–236. https://doi.org/10.1097/PSY.0000000000000168.

Suni, Eric. "20 Tips for How to Sleep Better." Sleep Foundation. Last updated July 22, 2025.

Williams, R. "Anger as a Basic Emotion and Its Role in Personality Building and Pathological Growth: The Neuroscientific, Developmental, and Clinical Perspectives." *Frontiers in Psychology* 8 (2017): 1950. https://doi.org/10.3389/fpsyg.2017.01950.

Yau, Y. H., and M. N. Potenza. "Stress and Eating Behaviors." *Minerva Endocrinologica* 38, no. 3 (2013): 255–267.

7. Repairing Trust and Healing Trauma

Bigelow, Ann E., and L. R. Williams. "To Have and to Hold: Effects of Physical Contact on Infants and Their Caregivers." *Infant Behavior and Development* 61 (2020): 101494. https://doi.org/10.1016/j.infbeh.2020.101494.

Dalia El Hady and Michael S. Kramer. "The Importance of Touch in Development." *Paediatrics & Child Health* 15, no. 3 (2010): 153–56. https://doi.org/10.1093/pch/15.3.153.

Dunn, Judy, and Jane Brown. "Affect Expression in the Family, Children's Understanding of Emotions, and Their Interactions with Others." *Merrill-Palmer Quarterly* 40, no. 1 (1994): 120–137.

Hawkins, Roxanne D., Chih-Hsin Kuo, and Charlotte Robinson. "Young Adults' Views on the Mechanisms Underpinning the Impact of Pets on Symptoms of Anxiety and Depression." *Frontiers in Psychiatry* 15 (2024): 1355317.

Jeon, Jeewon, and Daeun Park. "Your Feelings Are Reasonable: Emotional Validation Promotes Persistence Among Preschoolers." *Developmental Science* (2024): e13523.

Koukourikos, Konstantinos, Areti Tsaloglidou, Laila Tzeha, Christos Iliadis, Aikaterini Frantzana, Aristi Katsimbeli, and Lambrini Kourkouta. "An Overview of Play Therapy." *Materia Socio-Medica* 33, no. 4 (2021): 293.

Lee, Catherine M., and Karen A. Bax. "Children's Reactions to Parental Separation and Divorce." *Paediatrics & Child Health* 5, no. 4 (2000): 217–218.

Marshall-Pescini, Sarah, Franka S. Schaebs, Alina Gaugg, Anne Meinert, Tobias Deschner, and Friederike Range. "The role of oxytocin in the dog–owner relationship." *Animals* 9, no. 10 (2019): 792.

Petersson, Maria, Kerstin Uvnäs-Moberg, Anne Nilsson, Lise-Lotte Gustafson, Eva Hydbring-Sandberg, and Linda Handlin. "Oxytocin and cortisol levels in dog owners and their dogs are associated with behavioral patterns: An exploratory study." *Frontiers in psychology* 8 (2017): 1796.

Seligman, Laura D., and Thomas H. Ollendick. "Cognitive-behavioral therapy for anxiety disorders in youth." *Child and Adolescent Psychiatric Clinics* 20, no. 2 (2011): 217–238.

Shedler, Jonathan. "The efficacy of psychodynamic psychotherapy." *American psychologist* 65, no. 2 (2010): 98.

Sorin, Reesa. "Validating young children's feelings and experiences of fear." *Contemporary Issues in Early Childhood* 4, no. 1 (2003): 80–89.

Sunrise Residential Treatment Center. "Interpersonal Effectiveness: 4 Powerful

DBT Skills for Teens." *Sunrise RTC*. Accessed November 6, 2024. https://sunrisertc.com/interpersonal-effectiveness/.

Surma, Stanisław, Suzanne Oparil, and Krzysztof Narkiewicz. "Pet ownership and the risk of arterial hypertension and cardiovascular disease." *Current Hypertension Reports* 24, no. 8 (2022): 295–302.

Turunen, Jani, Annika Norell-Clarke, and Curt Hagquist. "How Do Children and Adolescents of Separated Parents Sleep? An Investigation of Custody Arrangements, Sleep Habits, Sleep Problems, and Sleep Duration in Sweden." *Sleep Health* 7, no. 6 (2021): 716–722. https://doi.org/10.1016/j.sleh.2021.06.002.

8. New Partners and Blended Families

Centers for Disease Control and Prevention. "Structure and Rules: The Importance of Setting Limits for Toddlers." Last modified June 29, 2021. https://www.cdc.gov/parenting-toddlers/structure-rules/structure.html.

Dausch, Elizabeth. "Ignoring Feelings." Elizabeth Dausch Therapy. Accessed September 27, 2024. https://www.elizabethdauschtherapy.com/blog/ignoring-feelings.

Freud, Sigmund. *Three Essays on the Theory of Sexuality*. Translated by James Strachey. New York: Basic Books, 2000.

Oolup, Craig, Jason Brown, Elizabeth Nowicki, and Danielle Aziz. "The emotional experience and expression of anger: Children's perspectives." *Child and adolescent social work journal* 33 (2016): 279–292.

Round, Alicia, William Baker, and Christopher Rayner. "Using Visual Arts to Encourage Children with Autism Spectrum Disorder to Communicate Their Feelings and Emotions." *Open Journal of Social Sciences* 5, no. 10 (October 2017): 90–108.

Spiegel, Leo A. "A review of contributions to a psychoanalytic theory of adolescence: individual aspects." *The psychoanalytic study of the child* 6, no. 1 (1951): 375–393.

9. Special Situations

Darnall, Douglas. *Divorce Casualties: Protecting Your Children from Parental Alienation.* Lanham, MD: Taylor Trade Publishing, 1998.

Eyden, Julie, Catherine Winsper, Dieter Wolke, Matthew R. Broome, and Fiona MacCallum. "A systematic review of the parenting and outcomes experienced by offspring of mothers with borderline personality pathology: Potential mechanisms and clinical implications." *Clinical Psychology Review* 47 (2016): 85–105.

Glynn, Laura M., and Tallie Z. Baram. "The influence of unpredictable, fragmented parental signals on the developing brain." *Frontiers in Neuroendocrinology* 53 (2019): 100736.

Honda, Tomoko, Thach Tran, Sally Popplestone, Catherine E. Draper, Aisha K. Yousafzai, Lorena Romero, and Jane Fisher. "Parents' mental health and the social-emotional development of their children aged between 24 and 59 months in low-and middle-income countries: A systematic review and meta-analyses." *SSM-Mental Health* 3 (2023): 100197.

Kamis, Christina. "The long-term impact of parental mental health on children's distress trajectories in adulthood." *Society and Mental Health* 11, no. 1 (2021): 54–68.

Petfield, Lara, Helen Startup, Hannah Droscher, and Sam Cartwright-Hatton. "Parenting in mothers with borderline personality disorder and impact on child outcomes." *BMJ Ment Health* 18, no. 3 (2015): 67–75.

Pierce, Matthias, Holly F. Hope, Adekeye Kolade, Judith Gellatly, Cemre Su Osam, Reena Perchard, Kyriaki Kosidou et al. "Effects of parental mental illness on children's physical health: systematic review and meta-analysis." *The British Journal of Psychiatry* 217, no. 1 (2020): 354–363.

Reynolds, Jenny, and Catherine Houlston. *Parental conflict: Outcomes and interventions for children and families.* Chicago, IL: Policy Press, 2014.

Rutter, Michael, and David Quinton. "Parental psychiatric disorder: Effects on children." *Psychological medicine* 14, no. 4 (1984): 853–880.

Stallard, Paul, Philip Norman, Sarah Huline-Dickens, Emma Salter, and Jan Cribb. "The effects of parental mental illness upon children: A descriptive study of the views of parents and children." *Clinical Child Psychology and Psychiatry* 9, no. 1 (2004): 39–52.

Wilkinson, K., S. Ball, S. B. Mitchell, O. C. Ukoumunne, H. A. O'Mahen, M. Tejerina-Arreal, R. Hayes, V. Berry, I. Petrie, and T. Ford. "The longitudinal relationship between child emotional disorder and parental mental health in the British Child and Adolescent Mental Health surveys 1999 and 2004." *Journal of Affective Disorders* 288 (2021): 58–67.

10. Is My Kid OK?

Child Mind Institute. "Disruptive Behavior: Why It's Often Misdiagnosed." *Child Mind Institute*. Accessed October 20, 2024. https://childmind.org/article/disruptive-behavior-why-its-often-misdiagnosed/.

Chu, Brianna, Komal Marwaha, Terrence Sanvictores, Ayoola O. Awosika, and Derek Ayers. "Physiology, stress reaction." In *StatPearls [Internet]*. StatPearls Publishing, 2024.

Higley, Elizabeth, and Mary Dozier. "Nighttime maternal responsiveness and infant attachment at one year." *Attachment & Human Development* 11, no. 4 (2009): 347–363.

Hoek, Hans Wijbrand, and Daphne Van Hoeken. "Review of the prevalence and incidence of eating disorders." *International Journal of eating disorders* 34, no. 4 (2003): 383–396.

King, Jean A., Russell A. Barkley, and Susan Barrett. "Attention-deficit hyperactivity disorder and the stress response." *Biological psychiatry* 44, no. 1 (1998): 72–74.

National Eating Disorders Association. "Eating Disorders in Men and Boys." *National Eating Disorders Association*. Accessed October 20, 2024. https://www.nationaleatingdisorders.org/eating-disorders-in-men-and-boys.

National Eating Disorders Association. "Statistics & Research on Eating Disorders." *National Eating Disorders Association*. Accessed October 20, 2024. https://www.nationaleatingdisorders.org/statistics/.

National Institute of Mental Health. "Eating Disorders." *National Institute of Mental Health*. Accessed October 20, 2024. https://www.nimh.nih.gov/health/statistics/eating-disorders.

National Research Council (US) and Institute of Medicine (US) Forum on Adolescence. *Sleep Needs, Patterns, and Difficulties of Adolescents: Summary of a Workshop*. Edited by Mary G. Graham. Washington, DC: National Academies Press (US), 2000. https://www.ncbi.nlm.nih.gov/books/NBK222804/.

Morris, Amanda S., Jennifer S. Silk, Laurence Steinberg, Sonya S. Myers, and L. Caitlin Robinson. "The Role of the Family Context in the Development of Emotion Regulation." *Social Development* 16, no. 2 (2007): 361–388. https://doi.org/10.1111/j.1467-9507.2007.00389.x.

Silvers, Jennifer A. "Adolescence as a pivotal period for emotion regulation development." *Current opinion in psychology* 44 (2022): 258–263.

WebMD. "ADHD Medication Side Effects in Children: Serious Problems." *WebMD*. Accessed October 20, 2024. https://www.webmd.com/add-adhd/childhood-adhd/adhd-serious-medication-side-effects.

INDEX

A

abuse
   evaluating child for signs of, 132
   by ex or ex's new partner, 119, 132
academics, in school, 100
acceptance, in mourning process, 61
accountants, 25
activating emotion, 78
addiction
   other forms of, 154
   substance abuse, 130–32, 154–55
ADHD or distractibility
   in adolescents, 70
   medication as superficial solution, 146
   as a slight response to stress, 145–46
   therapy for, 147
   treating symptoms of, 147
   in young children, 146
adjustment reaction, 141
adolescents
   aggressive behaviors, 145

   brain development, 9–10, 20
   custody schedules, 53
   effect of divorce on, 21
   18-year-olds, 23–24
   emotional development, 70–71
   emotional regulation, 145
   mental health, 4, 5
   need for control and independence, 53
   and physical affection, 95
   rapprochement process, 21
   reactions to new partner, 108–9
   sleep issues, 143–44
   therapy for, 19, 29–30, 98, 141–42
   worrying about parent's happiness, 109
adrenaline, 142
affection, competing for, 83
aggressive behaviors
   in adolescents, 145
   between siblings, 145
   in small children, 144–45
   in toddlers, 66, 144–45

Index

alcohol
  abuse, 77, 130–32
  addiction, 154–55
  to relieve stress, 74
alienation, parental, 79, 127–30
amygdala, 70
anger
  children's, 96–97
  misplaced, 17–18
  in mourning process, 60
  moving past, 77–79
  toward ex-partner, 80
  uncontrolled, 137
anorexia, 151, 153
anxiety
  childhood, diagnoses of, 5
  from chronic stress, 28
  cognitive behavioral therapy for, 98
  from conflicting loyalties, 56
  defined, 150
  effect on sleep, 74
  meditation or behavioral relaxation for, 75
  parents with, 133–34
  seeking professional help for, 90–91
  separation, in babies, 62
  signs or symptoms of, 150
  stress response to, 149
appetite, 74
arguments, winning, 84–85
attachment disorder, 62
attachment security, 7–10
attachment theory, 50
aunts, 89–90, 100, 121

B

bad moods, 100, 137
bargaining, in mourning process, 60–61
bed wetting, 95
behavioral relaxation, 75
behavioral therapy, 150
binge-eating disorders, 151, 153
blame, 80–82
blended family, 120–21
"bonus kids," 116–17
borderline personality disorder (BPD), 134, 135–36
boundaries, clear, 24
Bowlby, John, 50
brain development
  in adolescents, 9–10, 20
  in children, 12
  in infants and babies, 7–9, 20–21, 50
breastfeeding mothers, 49, 50, 51, 62
breathing exercises, 144
bulimia, 151, 153
business travel, 94

C

case studies
  adult bad moods, 137
  adult depression, 133–34
  adult mental illness, 135
  alcohol problems, 131
  anger over new partner, 115
  blaming ex-partner, 81–82
  children's sleep issues, 64–65
  children used as spies, 88–89

court-ordered custody, 54–55
custody for infants and babies, 8–9
custody schedules, 52
family trauma, 76–77
feeling anger toward ex-partner, 78–79
financial arrangements, 86–87
flexibility with custody, 85–86
isolating kids from extended family, 90
jealousy over new partner, 111–12
kids worrying about parent's happiness, 110
learning to coparent successfully, 6
marital conflict, 76–77
misplaced anger, 17–18
more time with father, 52
negligent ex-partner, 126–27
parental alienation, 128
parent coordinators, 48–49
remarrying, 118
school support systems, 68–70
second chance at parenting, 161–63
suicidal thoughts, 148–49
therapy for adolescents, 29–30
timing of divorce, 12–14
celebrations, 102
child-centered divorce
   anticipating conflicts and needs, 25–26
   being your best self, 16–18
   as better than bad marriage, 1–14
   building your support system, 18–20
   change as little as possible, 22–23
   communicating with your ex, 40–44
   effect on children's development, 6–7
   focus on children, 3
   giving child some control, 23–25
   making a plan for, 15–30
   tangible benefits of, 5
children. *See also* adolescents; infants and babies; toddlers
   absorbing their anger, 96–97
   access to extended family, 89–90
   acknowledging their feelings, 95–96
   addictions, 154–55
   aggressive behavior, 144–45
   anger toward new partner, 113–14
   anxiety, 149–50
   better off after divorce, 160–61
   "bonus kids," 116–17
   brain development, 12
   childhood stress, 2
   competing for affection from, 83
   custody preferences, 55–56
   depression and suicidal thoughts, 147–49
   disordered eating and eating disorders, 150–54
   distractibility or ADHD, 145–47
   emotional development, 6–7
   fantasies of parent's reunion, 105–6
   giving control over decisions, 23–25
   healing trauma, 93–103
   how much information to share with, 35–37
   how to talk about divorce, 31–40
   how to tell about divorce, 33–34
   introducing to new partner, 106–9
   jealous of new partner, 110–13
   mental health, 4, 5, 141–45

children (*continued*)
  and negligent ex-partner, 124–27
  oversharing with, 36, 87–88
  playing one parent against the other, 24–25
  questions from, 39–40
  reactions to divorce, 59–71
  reactions to new partner, 108–9
  refusing to accept new partner, 114–16
  regressive behaviors, 94–95
  repairing trust, 93–103
  resemblance to ex-partner, 82
  school-age (3 to 9), 12, 67–70
  sensitivity to parental conflict, 129
  signs of healing, 103
  signs of stress, 19
  sleep issues, 142–44
  stress management for, 99–100
  therapy for, 19–20, 97–99
  used as a messenger, 43
  used as spy on ex-partner, 88–89
  victims of parental alienation, 127–30
  when to tell about divorce, 32–33
  when your ex won't help, 155–56
  worrying about parent's happiness, 109
child support, 25
child welfare, 132
Christmas, 102
chronic stress, 28–29
cognitive behavioral therapy (CBT)
  breathing exercises, 144
  for eating disorders, 153–54
  for help with anxiety, 98
  meditations, 144
  for teens, 19, 144

communication skills, 37–39
conflicts and needs, anticipating, 25–26
containment, 31
control, need for
  in adolescents, 53
  in children, 23–25
coparenting
  healthy, effect on children, 6
  housing arrangements, 22–23
  infants and babies, 20–21
  small children, 7–9
  therapy for, 44
cortisol, 74, 95, 102, 142
cousins, 100, 121
criticism, 129
custody
  children's preferences about, 55–56
  decided by courts, 3, 10–11
  dos and don'ts, 56–57
  fifty-fifty, 47
  flexibility with, 83–84, 85–86
  forensics process, 47
  for infants and babies, 7–9, 20–21, 49–51
  litigating, 53–57
  most common arrangements, 50–51
  negotiating, help with, 47–49
  nesting arrangement, 22
  and new partner overnights, 107–8

D

dating, 105
defensiveness, 84
denial, in mourning process, 60

depression
  childhood, diagnoses of, 5
  defined, 147
  effect on schoolwork, 70
  exacerbated by conflicting loyalties, 56
  parents with, 133–34
  seeking professional help for, 90–91
  signs of, 68, 147–49
  therapeutic techniques for, 98
  worsened, by divorce, 28
dialectical behavioral therapy (DBT), 19, 98
disappointment, 40, 89
disordered eating, 150–54
distractibility or ADHD
  in adolescents, 70
  medication as superficial solution, 146
  as a slight response to stress, 145–46
  therapy for, 147
  treating symptoms of, 147
  in young children, 146
divorce. *See also* child-centered divorce
  and attachment security, 7–10
  best time for, 12–14
  children better off after, 160–61
  children's reactions to, 59–71
  common wisdom about, 1–2
  feelings triggered by, 5
  financial and social upheaval, 5
  good, as better than bad marriage, 1–14
  how to first tell your child, 33–34
  legal decisions and consequences, 45–57
  length of process, 10–11
  over past 50 years, 10–11
  as a second change at parenting, 161–63
  signs of delayed reaction to, 147–49
  statistics on, 1
  talking with children about, 31–40
  the three Ps, 26–29
  when children go to college, 9–10
  when to tell your child about, 32–33
"divorce buddy," 91
divorce court
  custody agreements, 3, 10–11
  litigating custody in, 53–57
  litigation process, 46–47
dreams, 143
drugs, 130–32, 154–55

E

eating disorders, 150–54
eating habits, 65, 74, 75, 100
emails, 41
emancipation, 23
emotional alienation, 128
emotional development
  adolescents, 70–71
  children, 6–7
  infants and babies, 61–66
  school-age children (3-8 years), 67–70
  toddlers, 63–66
emotional disregulation, 135–36
emotional legacy, 158
emotions
  activating, 78
  not acknowledging, 95–96

emotions (*continued*)
  regulating, 16–18, 27, 66, 67
  safe outlets for, 66
employers, 94
endorphins, 74
exercise, 74
ex-partner
  best ways to communicate with, 40–44
  blaming, 80–82
  children providing information about, 88–89
  children's resemblance to, 82
  disagreeing about child's mental health, 155–56
  discussing destructive behavior with, 129–30
  feeling anger toward, 78–79, 80
  living far away, 138–39
  marrying a new partner, 117–18
  with mental illness, 132–37
  negligent, 124–27
  new partner of, 119–21
  with substance abuse problems, 130–32
  talking about divorce with, 31–40
  telling about new partner, 107
extracurricular activities, 100

F

face-to-face conversations, 71
family, extended, 89–90, 100
family rituals and traditions, 102
family therapy, 98

father
  importance of, in young children's lives, 49
  as primary attachment figure, 3, 50, 52
  wife's rage against, 81–82
fatigue, 74, 100
favoritism, 120–21
feelings. *See also specific feelings*
  conflicting, 117–18
  expressing, instead of internalizing, 113
  hearing and validating, 70, 71, 95–96
  negative, letting go of, 158
  oversharing, 36, 87–88
  projecting, onto children, 124
  sharing, with therapists, 97–99
  unconscious, in dreams, 143
  venting, at home, 145
feelings chart, 66, 67, 125
feelings journal, 119
feelings-oriented psychodynamic therapist, 147
fight-or-flight response
  in adolescents, 70
  in adults, 74, 141
  in children, 67, 145
  in infants, 62
financial advisers, 25
financial arrangements, 86–87
flexibility in schedules, 83–86
food, 65
Foreman, Joshua, 5, 16
forensic psychologists, 46–47, 136
former spouse. *See* ex-partner

Freud, Sigmund, 110
friends, 75–76, 100
frustration, 67–68

G
gender neutrality, 10
grandparents, 89–90, 100, 121
gratitude, 163
Gross, Jillian E., 2, 5, 11
guidance counselors, 99

H
home schooling, 146

I
illness, 28–29
immune system, 28–29
impulsivity, 67–68
infants and babies. *See also* toddlers
    brain development, 7–9, 20–21, 50
    breastfeeding, 49, 50, 51, 62
    custody arrangements, 20–21, 49–51
    emotional development, 61–66
    primary attachment figure, 7–9, 20–21, 49–51, 62
    reaction to new partner, 107
    weaning, 51, 62
infidelity
    blame for, 81–82
    as factor in divorce, 36, 80
insecurity, 84
"I wonder" phrase, 96

J
jealousy
    of ex's relationship with child, 79–80
    of new partner, 110–13
journal writing, 119

K
King Solomon, 3
Kübler-Ross, Elisabeth, 59–60

L
lawyers, 32
legacy, emotional, 158
legal decisions, 45–57
listening, 37–39
litigation, 46–47, 53–57
love
    finding again, 164
    legacy of, 158
    talking with kids about, 111
    unconditional, 96
loyalty, buying, 83

M
Mahler, Margaret, 21
manipulation, positive, 41–42
marital conflict
    adverse effect on children, 2, 4
    case study, 12–14
    children's sensitivity to, 129
    divorce as an end to, 164
material things, 25, 83

Maudsley approach, 153
mediation, 32, 45–46
medical emergencies, 99
medications, 146–47, 150
meditation, 75, 144
melatonin, 143
Meltzer, Barnard, 27
mental health
   of adolescents, 4
   of children, 4, 141–45
   improving, with pets, 102
   mental illnesses, 132–37
   of parents, 90–91
   seeking help for, 97
mentalizing, 38
money, 25, 83, 86–87
mood swings, 137
mothers, breastfeeding, 49, 50, 51, 62
mourning process, 59–61, 81

N

narcissistic personality disorder (NPD), 134
needs and conflicts, anticipating, 25–26
nesting arrangement, 22
neurodevelopment disorders, 2
new partner
   bringing in too soon, 101
   child's anger toward, 113–14
   child's jealousy over, 110–13
   child's refusal to accept, 114–16
   extended family of, 121
   introducing to kids, 106–9
   marrying, 117–18
   overnight visits, 107–8
   playing favorites, 120–121
   trouble between kids and ex's partner, 119–21
nightmares, 63–64, 143
night terrors, 63–64, 143
nighttime security, 21
no-fault divorce laws, 10

O

oedipal victory, 110
oversharing, 36, 87–88
oxytocin, 102

P

parental alienation, 79, 127–30
parent coordinators, 41, 47–49, 130
parent guidance, in therapy, 20, 44
parents. *See also* coparenting; ex-partner
   for babies and toddlers, 20–21
   being flexibility in schedules, 83–84
   being generous with money, 86–87
   being manipulated by children, 24–25
   being your best self, 73–91, 164–65
   child as reminder of ex-partner, 82
   competing for child's affection, 83
   defensive, 84
   finding patience, 80
   having jealous feelings, 79–80
   marital conflict, 2, 4, 12–14, 129, 164
   moving past anger, 77–79
   oversharing with children, 36, 87–88
   primary attachment figure, 3, 7–9, 11, 20–21, 49–51, 62
   primary caregiver, 10, 20–21, 47

reaching out for help, 91
remarrying, 117–18
resisting the blame game, 80–82
secondary parent, 8
self-awareness, 76, 84
self-care and support, 73–76
signs of not being OK, 90–91
using child as spy, 88–89
winning arguments, 84–85
partners, ex. *See* ex-partner
partners, new. *See* new partner
pastoral counselors, 99
patience, 80
pause before speaking, 26–27
peace of mind, 28–29
perspective, 27–28
pets, 39, 102–3
physical affection, 95
play or art therapy
   about, 98, 143
   to address distractibility, 146
   to address sleep issues, 143
   best ages for, 19
   for disruptive behaviors, 69
Poller, Judith L., 10
positive manipulation, 41–42
power struggles over food, 65
prefrontal cortex (PFC), 70
primary attachment figure
   for babies and toddlers, 7–9, 20–21, 49–51, 62
   factoring into custody decisions, 11, 20–21, 49–51, 62
   fathers, 3, 50, 52
primary caregiver, 10, 20–21, 47
professional advisers, 19
professional financial advice, 25

promises, 40, 101
psychiatrists, 147
psychoanalysts, 143
psychoanalytic training institutes, 20
psychodynamic therapy
   about, 98
   for adolescents, 144
   for children, 143, 147
   feelings-oriented, 147
PTSD, 84
puberty, 70

R

rapprochement process, 21
reflective statements, 96
regressive behaviors, 66, 94–95
rejection, 89, 114
relaxation work, 75
remarrying, 117–18
resilience, 38, 50, 127
responsibility, taking, 96–97
rituals, calming, 75
rituals, family, 102
Rodriguez, Carmen, 2, 16
routines, 113

S

sacrifice, for children, 158–60
sadness, in mourning process, 61
same-sex marriages, 10
school, 146–47
   academic grades, 100
   counselors, 68–70
   phobia, 95
   social workers, 99

Second Chances (Wallerstein), 1–2
self-awareness, 76, 84
self-esteem, 76
separation anxiety, 62
separation issues, 95
Serenity Prayer, 94
sex, 36
Shapiro, Corey M., 16
sibling aggression, 145
side-by-side conversations, 71
sleep
   and adolescents, 143
   calming rituals for, 75
   detecting changes in, 100
   effect of anxiety on, 74–75
   problems, 142–44
   and separation issues, 95
   and toddlers, 63–65
sleep anxiety, 143, 144
sleep-wake phase delay, 143
socializing, 75
special situations
   ex-partner living far away, 138–39
   ex-partner with a mental illness, 132–37
   ex-partner with drug or alcohol problem, 130–32
   negligent ex-partner, 124–27
   parental alienation, 127–30
spouse, former. *See* ex-partner
stepparents, 114, 120–21
stepsiblings, 116–17
stress
   children's, 56
   chronic, 28–29
   from conflicting loyalties, 56
   developing resilience to, 50

   managing, 74–75, 99–100
   from marital conflict, 2
   and neurodevelopment disorders, 2
   processed in amygdala, 70
   signs and symptoms of, 19, 62, 74, 108
stroke-kick method, 42
substance abuse
   by children, 154–55
   divorce stemming from, 36–37
   by ex-partner 130–32
sugar, 75
suicidal thoughts, 145, 147–49
support system
   for adults, 91
   at children's school, 68–70
   creating a, 18–20
   friends, 75–76
   reevaluating, 100

T

talk therapy
   for mild anxiety, 150
   for suicidal thoughts, 148–49
   for teens, 19, 98
tantrums, 63, 95
teachers, 68–70
technology, and communication, 43, 138
telephone, 43
texting, 41, 138
therapists
   for adolescents, 19, 29–30, 98
   for adults, 17, 19, 32, 44, 91
   for children, 19–20, 69, 97–99, 130

therapy
  benefits of, 142
  play or art, 19, 69, 98, 143, 146
  talk, 19, 98, 148–49, 150
time, as commodity, 74
toddlers
  aggressive behaviors, 66, 144–45
  eating habits, 65
  regressive behaviors, 95
  sleep issues, 63–65
  tantrums, 63
transitions, 94
trauma
  healing, 93–100, 103
  overuse of word, 129
  unresolved, 76–77
trust, rebuilding, 101

U

uncles, 89–90, 100, 121
The Unexpected Legacy of Divorce (Wallerstein), 2

V

ventral striatum, 70
video communication, 43, 94, 138
visitation agreements, 49–53
visual feelings journal, 119

W

Wallerstein, Judith, 1–2
weaning, 51, 62
wine, 74
work arrangements, 94